SQE 1 PREP COURSE

ETHICS AND PROFESSIONAL CONDUCT

BY ANASTASIA & ANDREW VIALICHKA

2nd Edition

Published by MetExam
https://metexam.co.uk

Ⓜetexam

ISBN: 978-1-917053-34-1

Authors: Vialichka, Andrew & Anastasia Vialichka
Title: Ethics and Professional Conduct. 2025. 2nd Edition. SQE 1 Prep Course/ Andrew Vialichka & Anastasia Vialichka.
Description: 2nd Edition| London: MetExam, 2025.
Identifiers: ISBN 978-1-917053-34-1
Subjects: LCSH Legal ethics - England - Examinations, questions, etc. | Legal ethics - Wales - Examinations, questions, etc. | Professional conduct of lawyers - England - Examinations, questions, etc. | Legal education - Ethics - England. | Legal education - Ethics - Wales. | Solicitors - Professional ethics - England. | Solicitors - Professional ethics - Wales.

INTRODUCTION

Welcome to the threshold of your professional journey towards becoming a qualified solicitor in England and Wales. This text, intricately tailored as a vital component of the MetExam training course, is your gateway to mastering the Solicitors Qualifying Examination (SQE 1). It lays the foundation of your legal understanding and equips you with critical analytical skills essential for your success in the legal field.

Embarking on this journey, you are about to immerse yourself in the fundamental aspects of Ethics and Professional Conduct, crucial pillars of legal practice. This comprehensive guide is meticulously crafted to provide an in-depth understanding of the ethical standards and professional responsibilities governing England and Wales's legal profession. It is an essential resource for navigating the ethical dilemmas and professional challenges you will encounter as a solicitor.

In these pages, you will explore the essential tenets of professional conduct, from maintaining client confidentiality and managing conflicts of interest to upholding the integrity of legal services and ensuring compliance with regulatory requirements. The guide underscores the importance of ethical decision-making and provides practical scenarios to apply these principles in real-world contexts.

Throughout this text, authors draw upon a wealth of legal scholarship and case law. While specific contributions are not cited in the body of the book, a comprehensive list of all works referenced can be found at the end. These references serves as an acknowledgment of the significant works that have informed this text and as a resource for readers seeking to explore the subject matter further.

CHAPTER 1. ESSENTIAL PRINCIPLES

The Solicitors Regulation Authority (SRA) Principles are the core ethical standards that legal service providers, including firms and individuals such as solicitors, must adhere to. These principles serve as the foundation for ethical decision-making in the face of dilemmas.

Solicitors are obliged to conduct themselves in a manner that:

- **Supports the rule of law** and **proper administration** of justice.

- Maintains **public trust** and **confidence** in the solicitors' profession and legal services.

- **Preserves independence.**

- **Demonstrates honesty.**

- **Exhibits integrity.**

- **Promotes equality, diversity, and inclusion.**

- Prioritises the **best interests of each client.**

Consider a scenario where a client opts to name their solicitor as the executor in a will being prepared by the solicitor. This arrangement might serve the client well, especially if their affairs are intricate or if there is a likelihood of familial disputes. Nonetheless, appointing a professional executor, as opposed to a family member or another non-professional, could incur higher costs and might not be advantageous in straightforward cases like when the client's affairs are simple.

Before finalising a will that designates the solicitor as the executor, it is incumbent upon the solicitor to thoroughly discuss the alternatives with the client, ensuring that the client's decision is made with full awareness of the implications.

In instances where multiple Principles conflict, the Principle that protects broader public interest (such as the rule of law and a robust, secure market for regulated legal services) should be prioritised over individual client needs.

In pertinent situations, the solicitor must appraise their client of scenarios where their duty to the court and other professional responsibilities supersede their obligation to the client.

Solicitors must uphold professional integrity by ensuring that their actions align with legal and ethical standards. They should always act in their clients' best interests while maintaining independence, honesty, and transparency in all professional dealings. Misleading clients, the court, or third parties - whether through false statements, omission of key facts, or deceptive billing practices—is strictly prohibited.

Additionally, solicitors must foster equality, diversity, and inclusion in their practice. They should avoid discrimination, make reasonable adjustments for clients with disabilities, and ensure fair treatment of all individuals, both within their firms and in their interactions with clients. Compliance with these principles is essential to maintaining public trust in the legal profession.

QUESTIONS - CHAPTER 1

#	Question	Options
1	**What is the primary purpose of the SRA Principles?**	a) To regulate criminal law b) To establish ethical standards for solicitors c) To govern corporate law only d) To provide legal aid e) To regulate barristers only
2	**Which of the following is NOT an SRA Principle?**	a) Promoting equality, diversity, and inclusion b) Acting in the best interests of the client c) Maximising profit d) Upholding the rule of law e) Preserving independence
3	**A solicitor must act with...?**	a) Honesty and integrity b) Personal gain in mind c) Discretion only when necessary d) Total secrecy in all matters e) Only when legally required

4	**When two SRA Principles conflict, which should take priority?**	a) The principle that benefits the solicitor b) The one that serves wider public interest c) The one the client prefers d) The principle that incurs the least risk e) The principle that benefits law firms
5	**What must a solicitor do before accepting appointment as an executor in a client's will?**	a) Accept immediately if requested by the client b) Discuss alternatives and ensure the client makes an informed decision c) Decline the request due to conflict of interest d) Charge additional fees for legal oversight e) Appoint a family member instead
6	**How should a solicitor handle a situation where their duty to the court conflicts with their client's interests?**	a) Withdraw from the case immediately b) Prioritise the duty to the court and inform the client accordingly c) Follow client instructions at all costs d) Ignore the conflict if the client insists e) Seek guidance from another solicitor
7	**Which principle requires solicitors to maintain professional independence?**	a) Integrity b) Objectivity c) Independence d) Accountability e) Confidentiality

8   **What is the key profes-
    sional obligation when
    dealing with unrepres-
    ented parties?**

a) To act fairly and not
take advantage of their
lack of legal knowledge
b) To act only in the best
interests of your client
c) To offer them legal advice
d) To refuse to negotiate
with them
e) To direct them to the
court for legal guidance

9   **Under SRA Principles,
    what is the solicitor's
    duty towards client con-
    fidentiality?**

a) Confidentiality is absolute and never breached
b) It can be breached if
legally required or with
client consent
c) It is only required for
corporate clients
d) Confidentiality only
applies in criminal cases
e) It does not apply after a
case is closed

10 **A solicitor finds out that
    their client is engaging
    in fraud. What should
    they do?**

a) Maintain confidentiality
at all costs
b) Report it under their
duty to uphold the rule of
law
c) Ignore it unless the
court asks
d) Assist the client in cov-
ering up the fraud
e) Seek advice from the
Law Society

11	**What does "integrity" mean in the context of the SRA Principles?**	a) Adhering to moral and ethical standards b) Prioritising business success over ethics c) Acting in secrecy d) Following only statutory laws, not ethical codes e) Acting in a way that maximises firm profit
12	**A solicitor receives a valuable gift from a client. How should they respond?**	a) Accept it if it does not affect independence b) Accept it but declare it to the firm c) Politely decline to avoid conflicts of interest d) Accept only if it is monetary e) Accept it but reduce legal fees accordingly
13	**A solicitor must act in a client's best interests. When is this overridden?**	a) Never, as client interests always come first b) When it conflicts with legal and regulatory obligations c) Only in criminal matters d) When another client has a stronger claim e) When the solicitor benefits from a different decision

14	**What should a solicitor do if they become aware of a serious regulatory breach in their firm?**	a) Report it to the SRA b) Discuss it with the client first c) Ignore it unless it personally affects them d) Cover it up to protect the firm e) Resign and leave it unreported
15	**Which of the following best describes an "own interest conflict"?**	a) When a solicitor's interests conflict with a client's interests b) When two clients have conflicting interests c) When a law firm's policies contradict the SRA Code d) When a solicitor represents both parties in a dispute e) When a solicitor offers pro bono legal advice
16	**What is an example of a "conflict between clients"?**	a) Acting for both buyer and seller in a property transaction b) Representing a family member c) Providing pro bono legal advice d) Defending a criminal case e) Acting for a client who is a former employee

17	**If a solicitor must prioritise public interest over a client's case, what should they do?**	a) Proceed as instructed by the client b) Refuse to take the case c) Explain the limitation and act accordingly d) Withdraw representation without notice e) Take the matter to the Law Society
18	**What is the role of the SRA in legal practice?**	a) To regulate solicitors and ensure professional conduct b) To provide legal aid c) To prosecute all criminal cases d) To draft new legislation e) To oversee barristers exclusively
19	**A solicitor must promote equality, diversity, and inclusion. What is an appropriate action?**	a) Ensuring non-discriminatory hiring practices b) Refusing to act for clients based on personal beliefs c) Hiring based only on diversity quotas d) Offering discounted services to select clients e) Prioritising clients who align with firm interests

| 20 | **What should a solicitor do if a client's request conflicts with legal ethics?** | a) Follow the client's request to maintain good relations
b) Explain why the request cannot be fulfilled and refuse to act unethically
c) Ignore the ethical conflict d) Seek guidance from the client's family
e) Request a waiver from the client |

ANSWERS - CHAPTER 1

#	Correct Answer
1	b) To establish ethical standards for solicitors
2	c) Maximising profit
3	a) Honesty and integrity
4	b) The one that serves wider public interest
5	b) Discuss alternatives and ensure the client makes an informed decision
6	b) Prioritise the duty to the court and inform the client accordingly
7	c) Independence
8	a) To act fairly and not take advantage of their lack of legal knowledge
9	b) It can be breached if legally required or with client consent
10	b) Report it under their duty to uphold the rule of law
11	a) Adhering to moral and ethical standards
12	c) Politely decline to avoid conflicts of interest
13	b) When it conflicts with legal and regulatory obligations
14	a) Report it to the SRA
15	a) When a solicitor's interests conflict with a client's interests
16	a) Acting for both buyer and seller in a property transaction

17 c) Explain the limitation and act accordingly

18 a) To regulate solicitors and ensure professional conduct

19 a) Ensuring non-discriminatory hiring practices

20 b) Explain why the request cannot be fulfilled and refuse to act unethically

CHAPTER 2. ENSURING TRUST AND FAIR CONDUCT

2.1. NON-DISCRIMINATION

You are obliged to avoid any form of unjust discrimination that might influence your professional interactions and the manner in which you deliver your services.

A breach of this standard would occur if a legal firm explicitly stated on its website that it only represented clients in heterosexual relationships. Furthermore, legal firms are mandated to systematically monitor, report, and disclose workforce diversity data, in accordance with the guidelines set by the SRA.

2.1.1. ACCOMMODATIONS FOR DISABLED CLIENTS OR EMPLOYEES

It is your legal duty to implement suitable adjustments to ensure that disabled clients and employees are not significantly disadvantaged in comparison to non-disabled individuals.

Importantly, you must not transfer the costs of these adjustments to other parties.

It is critical to understand that these adjustments are required to be 'reasonable,' implying that a firm is not obligated to meet the needs of disabled clients and employees in every instance. For instance, if the cost of making such adjustments is excessively high, they may not be required.

Examples of reasonable adjustments might include:

- Facilitating **easy access to** the firm's premises for clients.

- Offering sign **language interpretation services**.

- Providing **specialised equipment** for employees with disabilities.

2.2. AVOIDANCE OF ABUSE OF POSITION

You are strictly prohibited from abusing your professional position to gain unfair advantage over clients or any other individuals.

Solicitors must not exploit their authority, knowledge, or influence for personal gain or to manipulate clients, colleagues, or third parties. Any action that results in undue pressure, coercion, or financial exploitation breaches ethical and professional standards.

Additionally, solicitors should remain transparent in all interactions, avoiding conflicts of interest that could compromise their duty to act in the best interests of clients. They must ensure that their advice and decisions are based solely on legal merit and ethical considerations, rather than personal or financial motivations.

2.3. HONESTY TOWARD ALL PARTIES

You have an absolute obligation to avoid misleading or attempting to mislead your clients, the court, or any other parties. This obligation can be breached not only through direct actions but also through failures to act, or by being complicit in the actions or inactions of others (including your clients).

In situations where the opposing party does not have legal representation, which is becoming increasingly common, it is essential for the solicitor to exercise extra caution to ensure that the unrepresented party is not misled.

Solicitors must provide clear, accurate, and truthful information in all professional dealings, ensuring that their statements, advice, and representations are not deceptive or ambiguous. Any misrepresentation, whether intentional or due to negligence, can undermine trust in the legal profession and may result in disciplinary action.

Furthermore, solicitors should actively correct misunderstandings if they become aware that a client, the court, or another party has formed an incorrect impression due to their statements or omissions. Upholding honesty is essential to maintaining professional integrity and the proper administration of justice.

2.4. FULFILLING UNDERTAK-INGS

It is incumbent upon you to fulfil all commitments (undertakings) you have made within the stipulated time frame. In cases where no specific timescale is agreed upon, these undertakings must be completed within a timeframe that is considered reasonable.

Similarly, legal firms bear the responsibility to ensure that all undertakings made by any member of the firm, including support staff, are duly fulfilled.

2.4.1. DEFINITION OF AN UNDERTAKING

An undertaking is characterised as:

- A **declaration**, either spoken or written, which may or may not explicitly use the term 'undertaking'.

- Made to a **party** who reasonably relies on it.

- A **commitment** that you or a third party will take certain actions, initiate specific proceedings, or abstain from certain activities. It's important to note that while a solicitor or firm is not obligated to provide an undertaking, once given, it must be adhered to.

Typical **Examples** of Undertakings:

- Securing title deeds from a lender to facilitate the sale of a property with an unregistered title at the land registry.

- Committing to pay the legal fees of the opposing solicitor. (Important: For the protection of the solicitor issuing the undertaking, it's advisable to have those fees already cleared in the client account when the undertaking is given. However, this is not a requirement for the validity of the undertaking, which remains binding regardless of the solicitor's current funds.)

- Agreeing to settle a mortgage from the proceeds of a property sale.

2.4.2. RECOMMENDED PRACTICES FOR UNDERTAKINGS

For best practice, an undertaking should ideally be:

- Issued **by a solicitor**.

- Provided in **written form.**

- **Explicitly intended** as an undertaking (for example, by starting with 'I undertake…').

- **Authorised** explicitly by the client.

- **Documented** in the client's file and in a central register of undertakings within the firm.

- **Unambiguous** in its terms—remember, any unclear undertaking will be interpreted against the giver.

Therefore, a **regulated person or firm should:**

- **Clearly define** who is authorised to give undertakings.

- **Establish** prescribed methods for issuing undertakings.

- Where feasible, **use standard undertaking forms** with strict guidelines for any deviations, subject to supervisory and management approval.

- **Implement** a system for having another fee earner review the terms.

- **Make sure** all staff understand the necessity of client agreement for undertakings.

- **Ensure** all staff are aware of the specific undertakings involved in land sale or purchase contracts and the requirements for completing such transactions.

- **Clearly outline** the process for monitoring compliance, maintaining a central record for oversight.

- **Attach a copy** of each undertaking to the relevant client file and clearly label the file.

- **Follow up** oral undertakings (given or received) with written confirmation.

2.4.3. COMMON PITFALLS IN UNDERTAK-INGS

Regrettably, undertakings can often be:

- **Issued by** any staff member in a legal firm.

- **Communicated** orally, often over the telephone.

- **Given** inadvertently, as the explicit use of the word 'undertaking' is not necessary.

2.4.4. UNDERTAKINGS BASED ON FUTURE EVENTS

In cases where an undertaking is contingent upon a future event, and it becomes evident that this event will not transpire, you have a responsibility to promptly inform the recipient of the undertaking about this change in circumstances.

2.4.5. RECORDING UNDERTAKINGS

Adhering to best practices, a legal firm is expected to maintain a robust system that keeps track of undertakings given and their subsequent fulfilment.

2.4.6. IMPLICATIONS OF FAILING TO HON-OUR AN UNDERTAKING

A solicitor is personally obligated to honour an undertaking, regardless of whether it was issued verbally or in written form. An undertaking is enforceable through the courts. The recipient of the undertaking has the right to seek reparation for any losses suffered due to its non-fulfilment.

While bodies such as the SRA, LeO, and SDT do not possess the authority to enforce an undertaking directly, any failure to comply may constitute a breach of professional conduct, potentially resulting in disciplinary actions against the solicitor.

#	Question	Options
1	**Which of the following is an example of unjust discrimination by a solicitor?**	a) Refusing to take a client due to a conflict of interest b) Charging different fees for different services c) Only accepting clients in heterosexual relationships d) Declining a case due to lack of expertise e) Offering a loyalty discount to repeat clients
2	**What must a firm do to comply with SRA diversity requirements?**	a) Nothing, diversity reporting is optional b) Monitor, report, and disclose workforce diversity data c) Only report diversity data when requested d) Hire employees based on quotas e) Ensure equal pay across all employees
3	**When is a law firm required to make accommodations for a disabled individual?**	a) Only if requested by the client b) Only if the firm has the financial capacity c) When reasonable adjustments prevent disadvantage d) Only if the client pays for the accommodation e) Never, as accommodations are voluntary

4   **Which of the following is an example of a reasonable adjustment?**

a) Refusing to take on disabled clients
b) Providing documents in Braille
c) Charging additional fees for accessibility services
d) Avoiding disabled clients to prevent inconvenience
e) Suggesting they find another solicitor

5   **What is considered an abuse of a solicitor's professional position?**

a) Using legal knowledge to mislead a client
b) Charging higher fees for complex cases
c) Offering free consultations
d) Refusing to represent a client
e) Hiring only qualified employees

6   **What should a solicitor do if a client provides false information?**

a) Ignore it
b) Report the client to the SRA
c) Advise the client to correct it
d) Continue representing the client regardless
e) Withdraw from the case immediately

7	**What is an undertaking in legal practice?**	a) A non-binding promise b) A legally enforceable commitment c) A standard contract clause d) A guideline for ethical behaviour e) An optional professional courtesy
8	**What must a solicitor do when giving an undertaking?**	a) Ensure it is in writing b) Only give oral undertakings c) Ensure it is enforceable by the SRA d) Seek client approval before issuing an undertaking e) Provide no documentation
9	**When must an undertaking be fulfilled?**	a) When the solicitor finds it convenient b) Within the agreed timeframe or a reasonable period c) Only when legally enforced d) Only if the client insists e) It does not have to be completed

10 **What happens if a solicitor fails to honour an undertaking?**

a) The undertaking is automatically void
b) The recipient can seek enforcement through the courts
c) The SRA cancels the undertaking
d) The client becomes responsible for fulfilling it
e) There are no consequences

11 **Who is responsible for fulfilling an undertaking issued by a law firm?**

a) Only the solicitor who gave the undertaking
b) The entire law firm
c) The client
d) The court
e) The SRA

12 **What should a solicitor do when giving an oral undertaking?**

a) Follow up with written confirmation
b) Rely on the verbal agreement alone
c) Ignore it if not documented
d) Cancel it if later inconvenient
e) Take no further action

13 **What is an example of an undertaking based on a future event?**

a) Agreeing to pay opposing solicitor's legal fees
b) Securing title deeds from a lender
c) Promising to settle a mortgage from property sale proceeds
d) Committing to take an action only if a certain event occurs
e) None of the above

14	**Who has the authority to issue an undertaking?**	a) Any staff member in a law firm b) Only a solicitor c) Anyone working in the legal industry d) Only senior partners e) Only barristers
15	**What is a solicitor's duty regarding honesty?**	a) Be honest only when required by the court b) Be honest at all times, including towards clients, courts, and third parties c) Be honest only in contractual matters d) Be honest only if it benefits the client e) There is no mandatory honesty requirement
16	**What is the best way for a firm to manage undertakings?**	a) By keeping a written record and ensuring compliance b) By issuing only oral undertakings c) By allowing non-solicitor staff to issue undertakings d) By keeping undertakings confidential e) By leaving it to individual solicitors to track their own

17 **What should a solicitor do if an undertaking cannot be fulfilled due to unforeseen circumstances?**

a) Do nothing
b) Immediately inform the recipient
c) Find another solicitor to fulfil it
d) Ignore the issue
e) Charge the client an extra fee

18 **Which of the following best describes an undertaking given by a solicitor?**

a) A promise that can be withdrawn at any time
b) A legally enforceable commitment that must be fulfilled
c) A voluntary assurance with no legal consequences
d) A general statement of intent
e) A client agreement subject to negotiation

19 **What is the consequence of a solicitor failing to fulfil an undertaking?**

a) The undertaking is automatically cancelled
b) The solicitor may face disciplinary action by the SRA
c) The client becomes responsible for the undertaking
d) The solicitor may simply issue a new undertaking
e) There are no consequences

20 **When dealing with an unrepresented party, what is a solicitor required to do?**

a) Take advantage of their lack of legal knowledge
b) Ensure that they are not misled
c) Provide them with legal advice
d) Avoid any communication with them
e) Treat them the same as a legally represented party

ANSWERS - CHAPTER 2

#	Correct Answer
1	c) Only accepting clients in heterosexual relationships
2	b) Monitor, report, and disclose workforce diversity data
3	c) When reasonable adjustments prevent disadvantage
4	b) Providing documents in Braille
5	a) Using legal knowledge to mislead a client
6	c) Advise the client to correct it
7	b) A legally enforceable commitment
8	a) Ensure it is in writing
9	b) Within the agreed timeframe or a reasonable period
10	b) The recipient can seek enforcement through the courts
11	b) The entire law firm
12	a) Follow up with written confirmation
13	d) Committing to take an action only if a certain event occurs
14	b) Only a solicitor
15	b) Be honest at all times, including towards clients, courts, and thii
16	a) By keeping a written record and ensuring compliance
17	b) Immediately inform the recipient

18 b) A legally enforceable commitment that must be fulfilled

19 b) The solicitor may face disciplinary action by the SRA

20 b) Ensure that they are not misled

CHAPTER 3. DISPUTE RESOLUTION AND LEGAL PROCEEDINGS

3.1. HANDLING EVIDENCE AND WITNESS TESTIMONY

3.1.1. PROPER TREATMENT OF EVIDENCE

You are strictly prohibited from misusing, tampering with, or attempting to tamper with evidence. Additionally, you must avoid any actions that aim to alter the substance of evidence, such as fabricating false evidence or inducing witnesses to modify their testimony.

3.1.2. GUIDELINES FOR WITNESS COMPENSATION

You are not permitted to offer or provide any form of benefit to a witness if such a benefit is contingent on the nature of their evidence or the outcome of the legal case.

However, reasonable compensation for expenses incurred, such as travel or accommodation costs, may be provided to ensure witnesses can attend court proceedings. Any payments must be transparent, proportionate, and not influence the content or credibility of the testimony.

Solicitors must also ensure that witnesses understand their duty to provide truthful and impartial evidence. Any attempt to induce or pressure a witness into altering their testimony can result in serious professional and legal consequences.

3.2. COURTROOM DUTIES

3.2.1. EFFICIENCY IN COURT

You have a responsibility to not squander the court's time. Ensure that all claims, assertions, or representations made to the court or other parties are well-founded and capable of being argued effectively.

This includes thorough preparation of legal arguments, adherence to procedural rules, and timely submission of necessary documents. Avoiding unnecessary delays and frivolous applications is essential to maintaining the integrity of the legal process.

Solicitors should also be mindful of courtroom etiquette and professionalism, ensuring that their conduct facilitates the efficient administration of justice. Clear, concise advocacy and cooperation with the court contribute to a fair and effective legal system.

3.2.2. ADHERENCE TO COURT ORDERS

You are required to abide by all court orders that impose duties on you. Additionally, you must avoid any actions that would place you in contempt of court.

Failure to comply with court orders can result in serious consequences, including fines, professional sanctions, or even imprisonment in cases of contempt. Solicitors must ensure that they understand and fulfil their obligations promptly and accurately.

If a solicitor believes that a court order is unjust or incorrect, the appropriate course of action is to challenge it through legal channels rather than ignoring or disobeying it. Maintaining respect for the judicial process is fundamental to upholding the rule of law.

3.2.3. DISCLOSURE OF LAWS AND IRREGULARITIES

It is your duty to inform the court of relevant legal precedents, statutory laws, and any procedural anomalies you are aware of that could significantly impact the outcome of the proceedings.

Failing to disclose relevant legal information or known irregularities can undermine the fairness of proceedings and may result in professional misconduct charges. Solicitors must act with integrity by ensuring that the court is fully informed of any material facts or legal issues that could affect the administration of justice.

Additionally, if a solicitor becomes aware of any procedural errors or misleading information presented in court, they have a duty to correct the record promptly to maintain the court's trust and uphold ethical legal practice.

CHAPTER 4. COMPETENCE AND PROFESSIONAL SERVICE

4.1. CLIENT INSTRUCTIONS

You are required to represent a client only based on instructions received directly from the client, or from a person who is duly authorised to provide such instructions on the client's behalf.

A corporate client may designate a specific employee, such as a legal officer or a company director, to provide instructions to a solicitor on the company's behalf. In this scenario, the solicitor should verify the employee's authorisation through company resolutions or other relevant documentation. This ensures that the individual is empowered to instruct on legal matters and can legally bind the corporation in accordance with its internal governance policies.

Failure to verify proper authorisation could result in legal complications, such as the invalidation of agreements or disputes over the solicitor's authority to act. Therefore, it is essential to maintain clear records of authorisation to protect both the solicitor and the client.

Additionally, when acting for vulnerable clients or those with diminished capacity, solicitors must take extra precautions to confirm that instructions are being given voluntarily and in the client's best interests, seeking independent assessments if necessary.

4.1.1. ADHERING TO INSTRUCTIONS FROM AN AUTHORISED REPRESENTATIVE

In cases where you receive instructions from a person authorised by the client, but have reasons to doubt whether these instructions truly reflect the client's wishes, you must refrain from acting on them. Only proceed if you are confident that the instructions accurately represent the client's intentions.

Acting When Client's Instructions are Unclear. In situations where it is not possible to obtain or determine the client's instructions, yet you still possess the legal authority to act on behalf of the client, your paramount duty is to safeguard the client's best interests. This requires exercising professional judgement and caution to ensure that any actions taken are aligned with what would most likely benefit the client under the given circumstances.

If there is any uncertainty regarding a client's instructions, solicitors should take reasonable steps to clarify the client's intentions, such as seeking further confirmation in writing or arranging a direct discussion. This helps prevent misinterpretation and ensures that legal actions align with the client's true objectives.

Moreover, if a solicitor determines that acting on unclear instructions could result in harm to the client's interests, they should document their concerns and, where necessary, seek guidance from senior colleagues or regulatory bodies to ensure ethical compliance.

4.2. DELIVERING COMPETENT AND TIMELY SERVICE

It is your responsibility to provide services to clients that are not only competent but also delivered within an appropriate timeframe.

Additionally, it is imperative to continuously maintain and update your professional knowledge and skills to ensure competence in fulfilling your role. This commitment to ongoing professional development is crucial in delivering high-quality legal services.

Failure to provide timely and competent service can lead to client dissatisfaction, professional negligence claims, or regulatory action by the Solicitors Regulation Authority (SRA). Solicitors must manage workloads effectively and seek assistance when necessary to ensure they meet professional standards.

Regular training, peer reviews, and staying informed about legal developments are essential for maintaining competence. Solicitors should also be proactive in addressing client concerns and providing clear updates on case progress to maintain trust and transparency.

4.3. PERSONALISED SERVICE FOR CLIENTS

You are required to take into consideration and respond to the unique characteristics, requirements, and situations of each client.

If a client has a hearing impairment, a solicitor should consider providing written communication or using text-based communication platforms, rather than relying solely on telephonic conversations, to ensure clear and effective communication.

Or

A client who is elderly and not familiar with digital technology might prefer face-to-face meetings or postal correspondence over electronic communication. In such cases, the solicitor should adjust their communication method accordingly to accommodate the client's comfort and accessibility needs.

Understanding cultural backgrounds, language barriers, and personal circumstances can also enhance the quality of service. Solicitors should be adaptable in their approach, ensuring that each client fully understands their legal matters and feels supported throughout the process.

4.4. MANAGING AND SUPER-VISING LEGAL SERVICES

4.4.1. OVERSIGHT AND SUPERVISION

When assuming the role of a supervisor or manager for others engaged in providing legal services, you retain accountability for the work executed through them. It is essential to provide effective supervision of the work being done for clients.

Firm's Supervisory Standards. It is mandatory for a legal firm to establish and maintain an effective system for the supervision of client matters. This system should ensure that all client-related activities are conducted competently, ethically, and in compliance with professional standards.

Supervisors should regularly review case progress, provide guidance where necessary, and ensure that less experienced staff receive appropriate training and support. Clear policies and procedures should be in place to uphold the firm's commitment to quality legal service and professional responsibility.

4.4.2. TRAINING AND PROFESSIONAL DE-VELOPMENT

It's your responsibility to make sure that the individuals under your management are equipped with the necessary competence to fulfil their roles. Furthermore, they should be encouraged and supported to keep their professional knowledge, skills, and understanding of their legal, ethical, and regulatory obligations continuously updated.

Similarly, a legal firm is obligated to ensure that all its managers and employees are not only competent in their respective roles but also remain informed and updated on their professional and ethical responsibilities. This duty encompasses a commitment to ongoing training and professional development for all staff.

Firms should implement structured training programs, mentorship opportunities, and access to relevant legal resources to support continuous learning. Regular performance evaluations and feedback sessions can help identify areas for improvement, ensuring that all legal professionals remain competent and aligned with the latest industry standards and regulatory requirements.

Additionally, firms should foster a culture of professional growth by encouraging participation in legal seminars, workshops, and certification courses. By prioritising ongoing education and skill development, firms can enhance the quality of legal services provided, maintain compliance with evolving regulations, and uphold the highest standards of ethical and professional conduct.

CHAPTER 5. HANDLING CLIENT FUNDS AND PROPERTY

5.1. RESPONSIBILITY IN ACCOUNTING FOR FINANCIAL BENEFITS

Should you gain any financial benefit due to following a client's instructions, you are required to accurately account for this benefit to the client, unless there is a prior agreement with the client stating otherwise.

This standard is equally applicable to firms, ensuring transparency and accountability in all financial dealings related to client instructions.

Failure to account for financial benefits properly may result in disciplinary action by the Solicitors Regulation Authority (SRA) and could lead to reputational damage or legal consequences. Solicitors must ensure that all financial transactions related to client instructions are clearly recorded, with detailed explanations provided to the client where necessary.

To maintain transparency, firms should implement strict internal controls and auditing mechanisms to monitor financial transactions. Regular training on financial accountability and ethical handling of client funds can help prevent errors, reduce the risk of misconduct, and reinforce a culture of integrity within the firm.

5.2. PROTECTING CLIENTS ASSETS

It is your duty to ensure the security of money and assets that are entrusted to you by clients and others. Legal firms are also bound by this standard, necessitating stringent measures to protect and manage any client funds or assets in their custody.

Failure to protect client assets can result in severe legal and regulatory consequences, including disciplinary action by the SRA and potential civil liability. Solicitors must establish robust safeguards, such as secure accounting systems, regular audits, and strict internal controls, to prevent loss, theft, or mismanagement of client funds.

Additionally, firms should implement clear policies for handling client money, ensuring compliance with the SRA Accounts Rules. Proper training for staff on financial management and fraud prevention is essential to uphold professional standards and maintain client trust.

5.3. MANAGEMENT OF CLIENT MONEY

You are not permitted to hold client money personally (meaning in your own business account as opposed to a designated client account) except in cases involving advance payments for fees and expenses.

In such instances, you must inform the client beforehand about where and how their money will be held.

Additionally, any funds held for disbursements should correspond to costs or expenses that you have incurred on behalf of the client and for which you are responsible, like fees for expert services. For more detailed information, refer to the Solicitors Accounts Outline.

Strict adherence to the SRA Accounts Rules is essential to ensure the proper management of client money. Solicitors must promptly deposit client funds into a designated client account and maintain accurate records of all transactions to prevent any risk of misuse or misappropriation. Regular reconciliations should be conducted to ensure transparency and accountability. Any discrepancies or issues related to client funds must be reported to the Compliance Officer for Finance and Administration (COFA) and, if necessary, to the SRA to uphold regulatory compliance and professional integrity.

#	Question	Options
1	**Which of the following actions would be considered evidence tampering?**	a) Presenting evidence that supports your client's case b) Encouraging a witness to alter their testimony c) Objecting to opposing counsel's evidence d) Failing to disclose privileged information e) Using expert witnesses in court
2	**What is a solicitor's duty regarding witness compensation?**	a) Paying witnesses for favourable testimony b) Offering benefits if the case is successful c) Reimbursing reasonable travel expenses d) Providing financial incentives based on the nature of testimony e) Withholding payment until after testimony is given
3	**What must a solicitor ensure when presenting a case in court?**	a) All claims are well-founded and capable of argument b) Arguments focus solely on the client's interests c) The case is prolonged to maximise legal fees d) Only evidence that favours the client is presented e) Judges are persuaded through emotional appeals

4 **How should a solicitor respond to a court order?**

a) Comply unless it is unfavourable to the client
b) Ignore the order if the client instructs otherwise
c) Challenge it by disregarding its requirements
d) Abide by the order to avoid contempt of court
e) Seek a delay without informing the court

5 **What should a solicitor do if they become aware of a procedural irregularity that could impact a case?**

a) Ignore it unless the client asks for disclosure
b) Inform the court of relevant irregularities
c) Use the irregularity to their client's advantage
d) Discuss it only with opposing counsel
e) Keep it confidential to avoid complications

6 **Who is authorised to provide instructions to a solicitor on behalf of a corporate client?**

a) Any employee of the company
b) Only the managing director
c) Any person authorised by the company
d) Any solicitor working on the case
e) Only the company's shareholders

7	**What must a solicitor do if they doubt whether an authorised representative's instructions reflect the client's true wishes?**	a) Proceed with the instructions to avoid delay b) Seek direct confirmation from the client c) Follow the instructions without question d) Report the issue to the SRA immediately e) Withdraw from acting for the client
8	**What is a solicitor's primary duty when client instructions are unclear but they still have legal authority to act?**	a) Delay action until instructions are received b) Make decisions based on personal judgment c) Act in the client's best interests d) Refuse to take any action e) Seek guidance from the court
9	**Why must a solicitor continuously update their professional skills?**	a) To improve their chances of promotion b) To meet legal regulatory requirements c) Only if instructed by their employer d) To ensure competitive billing rates e) It is optional unless mandated by the firm

10	**What is an example of a solicitor providing personalised service to a client?**	a) Using complex legal terms in all communications b) Relying solely on email for communication c) Adjusting communication methods to accommodate client needs d) Only accepting instructions in writing e) Refusing to make any accommodations
11	**When supervising others providing legal services, what is a solicitor's responsibility?**	a) Ensuring all work meets professional standards b) Leaving all responsibility to the firm's HR department c) Only supervising when issues arise d) Delegating supervision to administrative staff e) Assuming employees will self-regulate
12	**What must a legal firm establish for proper supervision of client matters?**	a) A system that ensures ethical and competent service b) A process that allows each solicitor to work independently c) A rotation schedule for supervision d) A separate team for non-legal tasks e) No specific system is required

13 **Why is ongoing training important for solicitors?**

a) To meet industry benchmarks
b) To ensure they remain competent in their legal practice
c) To increase billable hours
d) To maintain client loyalty
e) To stay ahead of competitors

14 **What is an employer's responsibility regarding solicitor training?**

a) No responsibility unless training is legally required
b) Ensuring all employees meet regulatory standards
c) Only providing training if requested by employees
d) Offering training at the employee's own expense
e) Only supporting junior solicitors

15 **What must a solicitor ensure before accepting client instructions?**

a) That the client has paid all legal fees upfront
b) That the client understands all possible outcomes
c) That the instructions come from the client or authorised representative
d) That the instructions align with the solicitor's personal beliefs
e) That the instructions are verbally confirmed

16 **What should a solicitor do when dealing with an elderly client unfamiliar with digital technology?**

a) Insist on digital communication only
b) Offer face-to-face meetings or postal correspondence
c) Require a family member to assist
d) Refer them to another solicitor
e) Only provide email communication

17 **What is an example of failing to adhere to court obligations?**

a) Making an argument in favour of a client
b) Failing to disclose relevant case law that contradicts a client's position
c) Presenting evidence to support a case
d) Cross-examining a witness
e) Filing legal documents on time

18 **Which of the following is NOT a responsibility of a solicitor in a legal proceeding?**

a) Ensuring courtroom efficiency
b) Misleading the opposing party to gain an advantage
c) Complying with court orders
d) Adhering to procedural requirements
e) Acting with integrity

19 **What must a solicitor do if they identify a procedural irregularity that benefits their client?**

a) Keep it confidential to protect their client's interests
b) Report it to the court
c) Use it to their advantage
d) Consult with the client before acting
e) Ignore it unless challenged

20	**Why is it important for a solicitor to confirm an authorised representative's authority?**	a) To prevent fraud and ensure legal validity
		b) To comply with client instructions without question
		c) To avoid unnecessary legal costs
		d) To satisfy professional curiosity
		e) To simplify case management

ANSWERS - CHAPTERS 3 - 5

#	Correct Answer
1	b) Encouraging a witness to alter their testimony
2	c) Reimbursing reasonable travel expenses
3	a) All claims are well-founded and capable of argument
4	d) Abide by the order to avoid contempt of court
5	b) Inform the court of relevant irregularities
6	c) Any person authorised by the company
7	b) Seek direct confirmation from the client
8	c) Act in the client's best interests
9	b) To meet legal regulatory requirements
10	c) Adjusting communication methods to accommodate client needs
11	a) Ensuring all work meets professional standards
12	a) A system that ensures ethical and competent service
13	b) To ensure they remain competent in their legal practice
14	b) Ensuring all employees meet regulatory standards
15	c) That the instructions come from the client or authorised representative
16	b) Offer face-to-face meetings or postal correspondence

17	b) Failing to disclose relevant case law that contradicts a client's position
18	b) Misleading the opposing party to gain an advantage
19	b) Report it to the court
20	a) To prevent fraud and ensure legal validity

CHAPTER 6. BUSINESS PRACTICES AND ETHICS

6.1. BUSINESS OPERATIONS AND RELATIONSHIPS

You are obligated to adhere to certain standards in situations where you refer a client to another person or entity, when a third party introduces business to you, or when you engage in fee sharing with a third party. These standards are also applicable to firms.

6.1.1. DISCLOSURE OF INTERESTS TO CLIENTS

When referring a client to another person, or when a client is introduced to you by a third party, you must disclose to the client any financial or other interests that you, your business, or employer may have in making the referral. Similarly, if the introduction is made by a third party, the client should be informed of any interest the introducer has in the referral process. This requirement is integral to maintaining transparency and trust in professional relationships.

6.1.2. DOCUMENTATION AND DISCLOSURE OF FEE SHARING

It's mandatory for any fee sharing agreements involving a third party to be documented in writing. Moreover, clients must be informed about any such fee sharing arrangement that pertains to their specific legal matter. This ensures clarity and consent in financial arrangements.

6.1.3. RESTRICTIONS ON PAYMENTS IN CRIMINAL CASES

You are prohibited from either receiving or making payments related to referrals, and from making payments to an introducer, specifically in cases involving clients who are subjects of criminal proceedings. This rule is vital to uphold the integrity of legal proceedings and to avoid conflicts of interest or ethical breaches in criminal cases.

Failure to comply with this restriction may result in serious disciplinary action by the Solicitors Regulation Authority (SRA). Solicitors must ensure that any business relationships or referral arrangements do not compromise their professional independence or create improper financial incentives.

Additionally, legal professionals should implement internal policies and conduct due diligence to prevent inadvertent violations of this rule. Maintaining transparency in all financial dealings is crucial to preserving public trust in the legal profession and upholding ethical standards.

6.2. RESTRICTIONS ON REFERRAL FEES

6.2.1. DEFINITION OF A PROHIBITED REFERRAL FEE

Under the current provisions of the Legal Aid, Sentencing and Punishment of Offenders Act 2012 (LASPO), the payment or receipt of referral fees in personal injury or death claims is strictly prohibited. This includes scenarios such as a solicitor paying a claims management company for referring a personal injury client to their firm.

The prohibition extends beyond personal injury or death claims to encompass any ancillary claims that arise from the same circumstances. For instance, an uninsured loss recovery claim resulting from the same accident would also fall under this prohibition.

6.2.2. PROOF OF COMPLIANCE

In instances where it seems to the SRA (Solicitors Regulation Authority) that you have either made or received a referral fee deemed prohibited, such a payment will be considered as such unless you can prove otherwise.

Consequently, it is crucial to maintain thorough records and management information. This documentation should be detailed enough to demonstrate that any payments you receive do not fall under the category of prohibited referral fees.

This requirement of proof and record-keeping applies equally to both individual solicitors and legal firms. It is a key aspect of maintaining transparency and adhering to regulatory standards in legal practice.

Failure to provide sufficient documentation may result in regulatory sanctions, including fines or suspension from practice. Solicitors and firms must proactively ensure that their records clearly outline the nature and purpose of any payments, including written agreements and justifications for transactions.

To further safeguard compliance, firms should conduct regular audits of financial records and implement internal policies to prevent inadvertent breaches. By maintaining robust documentation and transparent financial practices, solicitors can demonstrate their adherence to ethical and legal obligations.

6.3. DEALINGS WITH SEPARATE BUSINESS

A 'separate business' refers to any business that you either own, are owned by, actively participate in or control, or are otherwise connected with, and which is not an authorised body, an authorised non-SRA firm, or an overseas practice.

For the following actions, you must obtain the client's informed consent:

- **Referring**, **recommending**, or **introducing** the client to a separate business.

- **Dividing** a client's matter between your practice and a separate business, or **allowing** the client's matter to be so divided.

This standard is equally applicable to both individual solicitors and firms.

Consider a situation where a client requires assistance with estate planning, a service not directly provided by your legal firm. You may have connections with a separate business specialising in estate planning and trust services.

Before you can refer the client to this separate business, it is essential to obtain the client's informed consent. This includes explaining the nature of your relationship with the separate business and ensuring the client understands the scope and implications of the referral.

In such cases, it's also considered best practice to offer the client alternatives by suggesting more than one estate planning service provider. This allows the client to make an independent and informed choice about which service to use.

6.4. ADDITIONAL REQUIRE-MENTS FOR SOLICITORS

6.4.1. ASSOCIATION WITH AUTHORISED EN-TITIES

As an individual solicitor, you are required to ensure that any business affiliation you have aligns with regulatory standards.

Specifically, you must not hold a position as a manager, employee, member, or interest holder in any business that uses the term 'solicitors' in its name or implies through its description that it operates as a solicitor's firm, unless it is an authorised body. An authorised body, in this context, refers to an entity that has been officially recognised by the SRA (Solicitors Regulation Authority).

6.4.2. REQUIREMENT OF ANNUAL RETURN SUBMISSION

As a solicitor holding a practising certificate, you are obligated to complete and submit an annual return to the SRA (Solicitors Regulation Authority). This return must be in the form specified by the SRA. The annual return is a critical component of maintaining your status as a practising solicitor and ensures compliance with the regulatory framework governing the legal profession.

6.4.3. SECURING INDEMNITY INSURANCE FOR NON-COMMERCIAL LEGAL PRACTICE

When you are engaged in legal activities within a non-commercial entity, such as a not-for-profit organisation, a community interest company, or a trade union, and you undertake any 'reserved legal activities', it is essential to ensure that the entity secures and maintains appropriate indemnity insurance.

Although the requirement for insurance is triggered by the performance of reserved legal activities, it's important that the indemnity insurance provides sufficient coverage for all services you provide, irrespective of whether they are classified as reserved legal activities.

'Reserved legal activities' as defined by the Legal Services Act 2007, include:

- **Exercising a right of audience**, which involves the ability to appear before and address a court, including calling and examining witnesses.

- **Conducting litigation**, such as issuing, commencing, prosecuting, or defending court proceedings in England or Wales, and related ancillary functions.

- **Preparing instruments related to real or personal property**, for example, drafting any instrument of transfer or charge under the Land Registration Act 2002.

- **Preparing probate documents.**

- **Engaging in notarial activities**, traditionally performed by notaries.

- **Administering oaths.**

6.5. FIRM-SPECIFIC OBLIGATIONS

6.5.1. BUSINESS GOVERNANCE

Firms are required to implement and maintain effective governance structures, arrangements, systems, and controls.

These should be designed to ensure:

- **Adherence** to the terms and conditions of the firm's authorisation by the SRA (Solicitors Regulation Authority).

- **Compliance** by the firm's managers, employees, and interest holders with all the SRA's applicable regulatory arrangements.

- **Prevention** of any actions by the firm's managers, interest holders, and personnel, whether directly employed or contracted, that might lead to or significantly contribute to a breach of the SRA's regulatory frameworks by the firm or its staff.

- **Enablement** of the firm's compliance officers to effectively carry out their responsibilities and duties.

6.5.2. MAINTENANCE OF COMPLIANCE RECORDS

Firms are obligated to maintain comprehensive records that demonstrate their compliance with the regulatory arrangements set forth by the SRA (Solicitors Regulation Authority). This record-keeping is a crucial aspect of demonstrating ongoing adherence to legal and ethical standards.

6.5.3. ENSURING ACCOUNTABILITY

Firms must uphold accountability for compliance with the SRA's regulatory arrangements, even in situations where the firm's work is conducted by others. This includes the managers and employees of the firm, as well as any other individuals or entities with whom the firm enters into contractual agreements. This responsibility underscores the firm's obligation to ensure that all aspects of its operations, regardless of who is carrying them out, conform to the required standards.

6.5.4. RISK MANAGEMENT

Firms are required to proactively monitor their financial stability and the overall viability of their business. This entails the identification, monitoring, and management of all significant risks that could impact the firm's operations, including potential risks stemming from practices connected to the firm.

- **Procedures for Ceasing Operations.** In the event that a firm becomes aware of an impending cessation of its operations, it must ensure an orderly and systematic wind-down of its activities. This process should be managed in a way that minimises disruption to clients and maintains compliance with all relevant legal and regulatory obligations.

6.5.5. MANAGEMENT AND COMPLIANCE ROLES

(a) **Managers' Role.** As a manager of an SRA-authorised firm, you are charged with ensuring the firm's compliance with the Code of Conduct. In cases where there are multiple managers, this responsibility is shared jointly and severally among them.

(b) **Compliance Officers for Legal Practice (COLPs).** The **COLP** of a firm must:

- **Ensure** the firm adheres to the terms and conditions of its authorisation.

- **Guarantee** compliance by the firm, its managers, employees, and interest holders with the SRA's regulatory arrangements.

- **Prevent** actions by the firm's managers, interest holders, and those they employ or contract with that could lead to breaches of the SRA's regulations.

- Promptly **report** any serious breaches of the firm's authorisation terms or SRA regulations.

- Promptly **inform** the SRA of any facts or matters
  that should be reported for investigation of potential
  serious breaches or for the SRA to exercise its regulatory powers.

These duties do not extend to matters under the purview of
the firm's Compliance Officers for Finance and Administration (COFAs), as outlined below.

(c)   **Compliance Officers for Finance and Adminis-
        tration (COFAs)**

The COFA of a firm must:

- **Ensure** compliance with the SRA Accounts Rules by
  the firm, its managers, and employees.

- Promptly **report** any serious breaches of the SRA
  Accounts Rules to the SRA.

- **Inform** the SRA promptly about any facts or matters that the COFA reasonably believes should be reported for SRA investigation into serious breaches or
  to exercise its regulatory powers.

CHAPTER 7. MANAGING CONFLICTS, MAINTAINING CONFIDENTIALITY, AND ENSURING DISCLOSURE

7.1. ADDRESSING CONFLICTS OF INTEREST

Your foremost duty is to act in the best interests of each client.

However, if a conflict of interest arises, it may impede your ability to serve your client(s) effectively.

7.1.1. UNDERSTANDING CONFLICT TYPES

(a) **Categories of Conflicts.** Conflicts typically fall into two broad categories, which are:

- Conflicts between the solicitor (or firm) and the client, referred to as **'own interest conflict'**.

- Conflicts between two or more current clients, commonly known as **'conflict of interest'**. This is also sometimes distinguished as 'client conflict' to differentiate it from 'own interest conflict'.

Understanding these types of conflicts is crucial for maintaining professional integrity and adhering to ethical standards in legal practice.

(b) **Conflicts in Same or Related Matters.** Conflicts, or significant risks of them, often emerge in the same or related matters.

- **Conflict in the Same Matter:**

Consider a scenario where a law firm is representing four clients aiming to form a partnership. If these clients cannot reach an agreement on the distribution of profits, a conflict arises between them concerning the same matter.

- **Conflict in Related Matters:**

Conflicts can also occur in different, yet related, matters. A matter is considered 'related' if it involves the same asset or liability. For instance, a conflict exists if a solicitor plans to represent two companies both intending to acquire the same third company.

However, a general business interest does not necessarily create a conflict. A law firm can represent two companies in the same industry as long as the issues are unrelated. For example, advising one company on employment contracts and another on a litigation issue does not inherently result in a conflict.

However, the firm must remain vigilant about potential future conflicts (e.g., if one company decides to sue the other). This underscores the necessity for thorough conflict checks at the start of each new case.

(c) **Role of Other Solicitors in the Same Firm Regarding Conflicts.** In most cases, other solicitors within the same firm cannot act if a conflict is present. This is because conflict rules apply to the entire firm, not just to individual solicitors within it.

(d) **Timing for Conflict of Interest Assessment.** A solicitor must assess the potential for a conflict or significant risk of conflict at the very start of a matter, before any retainer is established. Furthermore, it's crucial to continuously evaluate the possibility of a conflict arising or intensifying throughout the duration of the retainer.

Consider a situation where you are representing a seller and a buyer in a property transaction. Initially, both parties have aligned interests: the seller wants to sell, and the buyer wants to buy.

However, as the transaction progresses, a dispute arises over certain terms of the property sale, such as the closing date or included fixtures. This dispute creates divergent interests between your two clients, leading to a conflict.

In this case, the conflict was not evident at the start of the retainer but emerged as the specifics of the deal were negotiated. This example demonstrates the dynamic nature of legal matters and the need for continuous assessment of potential conflicts throughout the client engagement.

(e) **Managing Situations When Conflicts Arise.** If you, as a solicitor, identify a conflict or a significant risk of conflict before establishing a retainer, the appropriate course of action is to refuse to represent any of the involved parties. Alternatively, you may choose to represent the client (or clients) whose interests you can best serve, ensuring that you do not represent any other client whose interests might conflict.

Should a conflict emerge during the course of the retainer, it is your duty to inform all involved clients. In such situations, you may find it necessary to stop representing all clients. However, it is possible to continue representing one party, being cautious of potential breaches in confidentiality obligations.

It's important to note that clients might not perceive the conflict as an issue and may wish for you to continue acting on their behalf despite the conflict. In such scenarios, you must adhere to professional standards and refrain from acting if a conflict exists.

- **Limited Retainer Options.** In cases where a firm identifies a conflict between clients, it might opt for a limited retainer. This means the firm will only handle aspects of the case where no conflict exists and will advise the client to seek independent counsel on the conflicted areas. The scope of the firm's involvement should be clearly defined in the client care letter (refer to Chapter 9 for more details).

- **Professional Embarrassment as a Basis for Non-Representation.** There may be situations where, despite the absence of a conflict or significant risk, a solicitor chooses not to act due to professional embarrassment. This occurs when the firm believes it cannot act in the best interests of a client, possibly due to factors relevant to the firm itself.

Suppose a law firm specialises in environmental law and often advocates for environmental protection causes. A new client approaches the firm for legal assistance in a project that, while legally compliant, is widely criticised for its potential environmental impact.

Even if representing this new client doesn't directly conflict with the interests of the firm's existing clients, the firm might choose not to take on the new client due to professional embarrassment.

This decision could stem from the firm's commitment to environmental values, and the concern that representing a client perceived as harmful to the environment could damage the firm's reputation and alignment with its core values.

7.1.2. HANDLING 'OWN INTEREST' CONFLICTS

An 'own interest' conflict occurs when a solicitor's duty to act in the best interest of any client in a particular matter conflicts, or there is a significant risk of conflicting, with the solicitor's own interests in that matter or a related one.

Examples of Own Interest Conflicts:

- **Financial Interest Conflicts**: Suppose a solicitor is handling a client's investment in a startup. If the solicitor also plans to invest in the same startup, this dual interest could hinder their ability to offer unbiased legal advice.

- **Personal Relationships**. If a solicitor is approached to represent a client in a divorce case, and the opposing party is a close friend of the solicitor, it would be prudent for the solicitor to decline the representation due to the personal connection.

- **Commercial Relationships**: If a solicitor is part of a firm that regularly provides legal services to a particular hotel chain, and a new client approaches the solicitor to file a lawsuit against that hotel chain, the solicitor should not take on the case due to the existing commercial relationship.

- **Employment Related**: A solicitor should not take on a case where the client wishes to sue the solicitor's previous law firm, where the solicitor had worked until recently, due to the potential conflict with the solicitor's past employment ties.

- **Solicitor's Conduct in the Matter:** If a solicitor accidentally discloses confidential information about a client to a third party, and the client considers suing for breach of confidentiality, the solicitor should not advise the client in this matter due to the direct involvement in the potential claim.

7.1.3. CONFLICTS BETWEEN CLIENTS

A conflict of interest situation exists when you owe separate duties to act in the best interests of two or more clients in relation to the same or related matters, and those duties conflict. There would obviously be a conflict if a solicitor acted on both sides of litigation or some other dispute between clients.

Other scenarios where a conflict of interest could arise include:

- Acting for both the seller and the buyer in a sale.

- Acting for both an investor and the scheme in which they will be investing.

- Acting for two clients who are agreeing to a commercial contract.

- Acting for clients who are seeking separately to purchase a particular asset or to be awarded a particular contract.

(a) **Adhering to Restrictions Unless Exceptions are Applicable.** You are required not to represent clients if a conflict between them arises, or if there is a significant risk of such a conflict, except in circumstances where one of two specific, limited exceptions is applicable.

These exceptions are narrowly defined and should be carefully evaluated before deciding to proceed with representation in situations where potential conflicts between clients are identified. It's crucial to ensure that any action taken under these exceptions strictly adheres to the applicable legal and ethical guidelines.

- **'Substantially Common Interest' Exception.** This exception is applicable when clients share a 'substantially common interest' in relation to a matter or a specific aspect of it. For this exception to apply, there must be a clearly defined common purpose among the clients and a strong consensus on the approach to achieving this purpose. The alignment of interests and objectives in the matter is key for this exception to be valid.

- **'Competing for the Same Objective' Exception.** This exception comes into play when two or more clients are in competition for the same goal, where achieving this goal by one client means it becomes unattainable for the others. In this context, an 'objective' refers to an asset, contract, or business opportunity that the clients are attempting to acquire or recover. This could be through a liquidation process, an auction or tender process, or a bid or offer that is not public. The exception allows a solicitor to act in situations where clients are vying for the same outcome in a competitive setting, provided certain conditions are met and the solicitor can navigate the inherent conflict of interests appropriately.

(b) **Conditions for Applying Exceptions.** If one of the exceptions ('Substantially Common Interest' or 'Competing for the Same Objective') is applicable, you may proceed to act for the clients only if all the following conditions are met:

- **Informed Consent from Clients:** The clients must give their informed consent, either verbally or in writing, for you to represent them. This consent should be clear and based on a full understanding of the situation, including any potential conflicts and how they might be managed.

- **Implementation of Effective Safeguards for Confidential Information:** In some cases, particularly in larger firms, it might be necessary to assign different fee earners to each client to ensure that confidential information is not inadvertently shared. This could involve physical separation (e.g., different buildings or floors) and distinct computer system access controls. However, if clients expressly wish for the same solicitor to represent them, safeguards might not be feasible. In this situation, the solicitor must carefully manage what information is shared between clients, based on explicit agreement from both parties, and obtain informed consent acknowledging that no safeguards will be in place.

Reasonableness of Acting for All Clients:

- You must be satisfied that it is reasonable to act for all clients involved. Considerations include:

- Whether all clients benefit from the joint representation (such as reduced costs or convenience).

- The extent of negotiations required between the clients.

The presence or absence of an imbalance in knowledge or bargaining power between the clients.

Consider a situation where you are representing two siblings in a dispute over the division of assets in their parent's will. Initially, the siblings agree to an equal split.

However, as the case progresses, one sibling begins to demand a larger share, citing past financial support given to the parents. This change creates a significant conflict of interest due to the evolving and unequal demands, making it potentially unreasonable for you to continue representing both siblings.

In a scenario where you are representing a startup seeking investment and a potential investor, if the negotiation is straightforward with mutually agreeable terms, there might not be a conflict.

However, if the investor starts imposing demanding terms that could jeopardise the startup's future (such as excessively high equity demands or unreasonable control over business decisions), this could create an imbalance, making it unreasonable to act for both parties.

7.2. UPHOLDING THE DUTY OF CONFIDENTIALITY

The duty of confidentiality is often regarded as the foundational element of the solicitor-client relationship. It is based on the principle that a client should be able to disclose any information to their solicitor with the assurance that it will remain confidential and not be shared outside of the firm.

7.2.1. ENSURING CONFIDENTIALITY OF CLIENT AFFAIRS

As a solicitor, you are obligated to maintain the confidentiality of your clients' affairs. This duty can only be overridden if (1) the law requires or permits disclosure, or (2) the client gives their consent.

(a) **Circumstances Where Disclosure Is Permitted.** Disclosure of client information is generally permissible in the following scenarios:

- When the client has given explicit consent for the disclosure.

- If a solicitor needs to disclose a client's will to an attorney appointed under a Lasting Power of Attorney, unless the Power explicitly prohibits such disclosure.

- In cases where the client is using the solicitor to commit a crime or fraud.

- If there is a statutory requirement for disclosure, such as the need to reveal tax affairs to HM Revenue and Customs.

- Under statutory duties, for example, under anti-money laundering regulations.

- When there is a court order or a police warrant that mandates disclosure.

(b) Situations Where a Breach Might Be Justifiable. Although disclosure without client consent is generally prohibited unless legally mandated, there are certain exceptional circumstances where a solicitor's breach of confidentiality might be justified to prevent harm.

These include:

- Preventing the commission of a criminal offence that could result in serious bodily harm.

- Cases where the client has expressed intentions of suicide or serious self-harm.

- Protecting a child or vulnerable adult from harm.

It's important to note that disclosure made post-event (e.g., after an injury has occurred) is not justifiable under these exceptions.

7.2.2. SCOPE OF THE DUTY OF CONFIDENTIALITY

This duty extends to every member of the firm, not solely the solicitor directly handling the case. All personnel, including support staff, consultants, locums, and others working in the firm or in-house practice, are bound by the duty of confidentiality towards the firm's clients.

This comprehensive application ensures that client confidentiality is upheld at all levels of the firm's operations.

Imagine you had previously provided legal counsel to a client regarding a sensitive business negotiation that involved trade secrets. Even after the client's passing, you should not disclose any details of these discussions or the nature of the trade secrets to anyone, including other parties interested in the negotiation.

The duty of confidentiality persists, and the right to waive or enforce this duty now lies with the client's personal representatives. This scenario highlights the enduring nature of confidentiality obligations, maintaining the sanctity of client trust beyond their lifetime.

7.2.3. DIFFERENTIATING CONFIDENTIALITY FROM LEGAL PROFESSIONAL PRIVILEGE (LPP)

It is crucial to understand the distinction between the duty of confidentiality and legal professional privilege (LPP). While both concepts deal with the protection of client information, they operate differently:

- **Legal Professional Privilege**: LPP specifically safeguards confidential communications between solicitors/barristers and their clients, primarily aimed at obtaining or providing legal advice. Such privileged communications cannot be disclosed or produced, even in legal proceedings, without the client's consent. This protection is absolute.

- **Duty of Confidentiality:** This duty has a broader scope, encompassing all confidential information regarding a client's affairs, not just communications for legal advice. While the duty of confidentiality allows for certain exceptions where disclosure might be permitted or required, LPP does not provide for such exceptions. Therefore, if information falls under the category of privileged communication, it remains protected under LPP and cannot be disclosed, regardless of the circumstances surrounding the duty of confidentiality.

7.2.4. IMPLEMENTING SYSTEMS FOR CONFIDENTIALITY PROTECTION

You are expected to establish and maintain effective systems and controls that help in identifying and mitigating risks to client confidentiality. These systems should be tailored to fit the size and complexity of your firm or in-house practice and the nature of the work you undertake.

When considering outsourcing services, ensure that the provider is committed to and capable of protecting your clients' confidential information adequately.

7.2.5. IMPLICATIONS OF BREACHING CONFIDENTIALITY

Violating the duty of confidentiality constitutes a breach of professional conduct. Such a breach can lead to disciplinary actions by the SRA (Solicitors Regulation Authority) or the SDT (Solicitors Disciplinary Tribunal). Additionally, the client affected by the breach has the right to take legal action against the solicitor for violating this duty.

7.2.6. PROFESSIONAL EMBARRASSMENT IN CONFIDENTIALITY MATTERS

Similar to situations involving conflicts of interest, there may be instances where, despite technically being able to act, a solicitor may choose not to do so due to professional embarrassment, especially in cases with potential confidentiality issues.

Consider a scenario where a firm is approached to handle a legal matter for a corporation.

However, the firm is already representing an individual in a separate matter who has confidentially disclosed information critical to the corporation's interests. Although there may not be a direct breach of confidentiality in representing both parties, the firm might choose not to represent the corporation to avoid the awkward position of holding sensitive information that could indirectly affect the representation.

This decision, driven by professional embarrassment, underscores the complexities of managing confidential information within legal practice.

7.3. UPHOLDING THE DUTY OF DISCLOSURE

The duty of disclosure mandates that any individual advising a client must inform the client of all material information relevant to the retainer, provided the advisor is aware of it. This duty ensures that clients are fully informed and can make decisions based on complete and accurate information.

7.3.1. CIRCUMSTANCES EXEMPTING DISCLOSURE

There are specific situations where you are not obliged to disclose information to a client:

- **Informed Consent for Non-Disclosure:** If the client has explicitly consented, in writing, to not being informed about certain information.

- **Risk of Harm:** If you believe that disclosing the information would result in serious physical or mental harm to an individual.

- **Legal Restrictions for Security or Crime Prevention:** If legal provisions, particularly related to national security or crime prevention (such as anti-money laundering or anti-terrorism laws), prevent you from sharing the information with the client.

- **Privileged Information Mistakenly Received:** If your knowledge of the information is solely due to privileged documents that were inadvertently disclosed to you. In such cases, the privileged nature of the documents takes precedence over the duty of disclosure.

7.4. MANAGING CONFIDENTI-ALITY VS. DISCLOSURE IN CONFLICT SITUATIONS

In situations where a conflict arises between confidentiality and the duty of disclosure, particularly involving current or former clients, specific guidelines must be followed.

You should not represent Client A in a matter where A's interests are adverse to those of Client B, a current or former client, if you or your firm hold confidential information about B that is material to A's case, unless one of the following conditions is met:

- **Implementation of Effective Safeguards:** Structural measures are in place ensuring that there is no real risk of the confidential information being disclosed. For instance, the team working for Client A does not have access to Client B's files.

- **Informed Consent from Client B:** Client B has given their informed consent, in writing, for you to act for Client A. This consent includes any measures taken to protect their confidential information.

Let's consider a situation where Client A approaches your firm for advice on acquiring a small business. You are aware that this business is currently facing undisclosed regulatory compliance issues, information you obtained while previously representing the business owner, Client B, in a separate matter. The knowledge of these compliance issues is crucial for Client A's decision-making process regarding the acquisition.

However, revealing this information would constitute a breach of your duty of confidentiality to Client B. In this situation, unless Client B consents to you disclosing this information to Client A, you must refrain from doing so and carefully assess whether it is appropriate to continue representing Client A in the acquisition.

CHAPTER 8. COLLABORATION AND RESPONSIBILITY STANDARDS

8.1. UPHOLDING THE DUTY TO CO-OPERATE

- **Compliance with Laws and Regulations:** You are required to stay informed about and comply with the laws and regulations that govern your professional conduct and practice. This includes keeping abreast of changes in legislation and regulatory guidelines that affect how you should operate within the legal profession.

- **Cooperation with the SRA and Other Regulators:** You must cooperate with the Solicitors Regulation Authority (SRA) and other regulators or ombudsmen who oversee or investigate issues related to legal services. This cooperation is fundamental to maintaining the integrity of the legal profession and ensuring that standards are upheld.

- **Prevention of Obstruction and Retaliation:** You are prohibited from attempting to prevent anyone from providing information to the SRA or other bodies with regulatory, supervisory, investigative, or prosecutory functions in the public interest. This includes a prohibition on any form of detrimental treatment towards individuals who provide or propose to provide such information. This aspect of the standard is crucial for fostering an environment where issues can be reported and addressed without fear of retribution or negative consequences. It is essential that concerns and complaints related to legal services can be freely communicated to regulatory bodies to ensure accountability and the continued trust in the legal system.

8.2. INTERACTIONS WITH THE SRA

As part of your professional duties, it is crucial to not only comply with the regulatory arrangements set by the Solicitors Regulation Authority (SRA) but also to be able to justify your actions as compliant.

In this context, your responsibilities include:

- **Providing Full and Accurate Responses:** When the SRA requests information or documents, you must provide comprehensive and accurate explanations, information, and documentation. This requirement is vital to demonstrate your adherence to the SRA's standards and to facilitate any investigations or inquiries the SRA may be conducting.

- **Making Information Available for Inspection:** You must ensure that all relevant information, whether held by you or by third parties acting on your behalf, is accessible for SRA inspection. This includes any information critical to the delivery of your legal services. The availability of this information is key to allowing the SRA to effectively oversee and ensure the proper conduct of legal professionals and firms.

8.3. REQUIREMENT FOR PROMPT REMEDIAL ACTION

As a solicitor or legal firm, you are required to take swift and appropriate remedial action when such action is requested by the Solicitors Regulation Authority (SRA).

This duty underscores the importance of responding effectively and promptly to any issues or concerns identified by the SRA, ensuring that any potential harm is mitigated and compliance with regulatory standards is maintained or restored. Quick and constructive response to the SRA's directives is essential for upholding the integrity and accountability of the legal profession.

8.4. OBLIGATION TO NOTIFY THE SRA OF SPECIFIC EVENTS

8.4.1. NOTIFICATION REQUIREMENTS FOR SOLICITORS

As a solicitor, you have a duty to inform the Solicitors Regulation Authority (SRA) promptly in the event of any of the following circumstances:

- **Criminal Charges or Convictions:** If you are charged with, convicted of, or cautioned for a criminal offence, you must notify the SRA. This requirement is subject to the provisions of the Rehabilitation of Offenders Act 1974.

- **Insolvency Events:** You are required to report to the SRA if you experience any relevant insolvency event. This includes events like bankruptcy or entering into an Individual Voluntary Arrangement (IVA).

- **Changes to Previously Provided Information:** If you become aware of any significant changes to information about yourself or your practice that was previously submitted to the SRA, and if this information is now or potentially false, misleading, incomplete, or inaccurate, you must notify the SRA. This ensures that the SRA has the most current and accurate information, which is essential for effective regulation and oversight of legal professionals.

8.4.2. REPORTING AND NOTIFICATION REQUIREMENTS FOR FIRMS

Firms have specific obligations to provide information and notify the Solicitors Regulation Authority (SRA) of certain events:

(a) **Annual Information Report:** Firms are required to submit an information report to the SRA on an annual basis or as otherwise specified by the SRA. This report is essential for the SRA to monitor and regulate the firm's activities and compliance with legal and ethical standards.

(b) **Prompt Notification of Specific Circumstances:** Firms must promptly inform the SRA in the following situations:

- **Serious Financial Difficulty:** If there are any indicators that the firm is experiencing significant financial difficulties, this must be reported to the SRA.

- **Insolvency Events:** Any insolvency events involving the firm, such as entering into administration or liquidation, must be reported.

- **Ceasing Operations:** If the firm intends to or becomes aware that it will stop operating as a legal business, the SRA must be informed.

- **Changes in the Register:** Any modifications to the information recorded in the SRA's register about the firm should be promptly communicated to the SRA.

- **Material Changes in Previously Provided Information:** If the firm becomes aware of any material changes to information previously provided to the SRA about the firm or its managers, owners, or compliance officers, and if this information could now be considered false, misleading, incomplete, or inaccurate, the firm must notify the SRA.

8.5. DUTY TO REPORT ACTUAL AND POTENTIAL BREACHES

As a legal professional, you have a significant responsibility to report both actual and potential breaches of regulatory arrangements:

- **Obligation to Report Serious Breaches:** If you become aware that any person or entity (including yourself) has committed a serious breach of regulatory arrangements, you are required to ensure that a prompt report is made to the SRA or another appropriate approved regulator. This includes reporting any facts or matters that you reasonably believe could constitute a serious breach.

- **Responding to SRA Inquiries:** If the SRA requests you to conduct an investigation into potential serious breaches, you must comply with this request and carry out the necessary investigation.

- **Reporting Suspected Breaches:** Even in cases where you may not have complete information to conclusively determine if a serious breach has occurred, you have an independent obligation to promptly inform the SRA of any facts or matters that you believe warrant its attention. This enables the SRA to investigate and determine if a serious breach has occurred or to take other regulatory actions as necessary.

8.5.1. UNDERSTANDING 'SERIOUS BREACH' IN THE SRA CONTEXT

The term 'serious breach' is not specifically defined in the SRA Code, as the SRA believes that a rigid definition may not be beneficial. However, the SRA's Enforcement Strategy, which complements the Standards and Regulations, provides insights into what constitutes a serious breach.

Such breaches typically involve:

- **Abuse of Trust:** Misusing the trust placed in you by clients or others.

- **Dishonesty:** Engaging in deceitful or fraudulent behaviour.

- **Unfair Advantage:** Exploiting clients or others for personal gain.

- **Misuse of Client Money:** Inappropriately handling or using client funds.

- **Sexual or Violent Misconduct:** Engaging in behaviour that is sexually inappropriate or violent.

- **Criminal Behaviour:** Conduct that is criminal in nature.

Aggravating Factors Indicating Seriousness:

- Deliberately or recklessly **ignoring** professional obligations.

- Demonstrating a **lack** of honesty or integrity.

- Exploiting someone's **vulnerability**.

- Causing foreseeable **harm** through one's conduct.

- Repeated **misconduct**, suggesting a pattern of irresponsible or unethical behaviour.

Consider a situation where a solicitor repeatedly fails to inform clients of significant developments in their cases, resulting in missed opportunities or detrimental outcomes for the clients.

While a single instance of failing to communicate might not necessarily be a 'serious breach', a pattern of such behaviour, showing a consistent lack of diligence and disregard for client welfare, could be considered a serious breach.

This pattern demonstrates a failure to uphold professional standards and responsibilities, thereby warranting a report to the SRA.

8.6. INDIRECT REPORTING TO THE SRA

In situations where you have an obligation to report information to the Solicitors Regulation Authority (SRA), it is acceptable to fulfil this duty indirectly.

You can meet your reporting obligation by providing the relevant information to your firm's Compliance Officer for Legal Practice (COLP) or Compliance Officer for Finance and Administration (COFA), as applicable. This approach is based on the understanding that the COLP or COFA will then relay the information to the SRA.

This provision allows for a more streamlined and organised process within firms for handling and reporting compliance-related matters to the SRA.

It ensures that information is channelled through designated officers who are responsible for maintaining regulatory compliance, thereby facilitating effective communication with the SRA while adhering to internal protocols.

8.7. RESPONSIBILITY TO ADMIT MISTAKES TO CLIENTS

In your legal practice, it's imperative to maintain honesty and transparency with your clients, especially when errors occur. Here are your key responsibilities in such situations:

- **Acknowledging and Addressing Errors:** If your actions or oversights result in loss or harm to a client, you are obliged to acknowledge the mistake and take steps to rectify the situation, if possible.

- **Full and Prompt Disclosure:** You must provide a thorough and swift explanation to the client about what went wrong and the potential consequences or impact of the error. This disclosure is crucial for maintaining trust and upholding the integrity of your professional relationship.

- **Cooperating with SRA Inquiries:** If the Solicitors Regulation Authority (SRA) requests, you need to conduct an investigation into whether there might be any claims against you due to the mistake. Following this investigation, you are required to submit a report of your findings to the SRA. Furthermore, it is your duty to notify any relevant parties who might have a claim against you as a result of the error.

CHAPTER 9. STANDARDS FOR PROVIDING SERVICES TO THE PUBLIC

9.1. CLARITY IN CLIENT REPRESENTATION

It is essential to clearly establish and identify who you are representing in any legal matter. This clarity is crucial for avoiding conflicts of interest and for ensuring transparent and ethical legal practice.

Misidentifying or failing to clarify client representation can lead to ethical breaches and legal disputes. Solicitors must explicitly confirm their role and responsibilities **in writing**, ensuring that clients understand the scope of representation from the outset.

In cases involving multiple parties, solicitors should take **extra precautions** to prevent misunderstandings. Clear documentation and communication help protect both the solicitor and the client while upholding professional standards.

9.2. COMMUNICATION ABOUT REGULATION AND PROTECTION

- **Informing Clients about Regulation:** Clients must be informed about the regulatory status of the services you provide. This involves clarifying which aspects of your service are regulated and how this impacts the protections available to the client.

- **Differentiating Regulated and Non-Regulated Services:** Make sure to distinguish between activities carried out by you as a regulated individual and those that are unregulated. This distinction helps clients understand the scope and nature of the legal protections and standards that apply to different parts of the service they receive.

- **Accurate Representation of Regulation:** It's important to accurately represent the regulatory status of any business or employer, including any separate businesses you may have. Incorrectly stating that a business is regulated by the SRA when it is not can lead to misunderstandings about the level of oversight and protection provided to the client.

9.3. ENSURING CLIENT AWARENESS AND UNDER- STANDING

9.3.1. CLEAR COMMUNICATION ABOUT LEGAL SERVICES

- **Accessible Information:** It is your responsibility to provide clients with information in a format and language that is easily understandable to them. This is especially important when dealing with legal concepts or procedures that may be unfamiliar to clients.

- **Empowering Informed Decisions:** Clients should be equipped with all the necessary information to make informed choices regarding the legal services they require. This includes understanding the nature of the services, how their particular matter will be managed, and the various options or courses of action available to them.

The aim of this standard is to promote transparency in legal services and empower clients by ensuring they have a clear understanding of their legal situation, the services being provided, and the implications of their decisions. This approach fosters trust and confidence in the solicitor-client relationship and contributes to the overall effectiveness of the legal representation.

9.3.2. TRANSPARENCY IN PRICING AND COSTS

- **Providing Clear Pricing Information:** It is essential to offer clients the clearest possible information regarding how their matter will be priced. This includes an explanation of your fee structure, whether it's based on an hourly rate, a fixed fee, a contingency basis, or any other pricing model.

- **Ongoing Cost Communication:** Clients must also receive comprehensive information about the likely overall cost of their case, both at the outset of your engagement and, importantly, as the matter progresses. This should include regular updates on costs incurred and any changes in the cost estimate due to evolving circumstances or unforeseen developments in their case.

Imagine a solicitor is representing a client in a property dispute and initially estimates the legal fees to be around £3,000 plus VAT. As the case progresses, it becomes clear that expert witness testimony is needed, which was not anticipated at the outset. This additional requirement will increase the legal fees by £1,500 plus VAT. The solicitor must promptly inform the client of this revised estimate, bringing the total expected cost to £4,500 plus VAT.

It is crucial for the solicitor to communicate this increase to the client as soon as possible, rather than waiting until the case concludes and the final bill is prepared. This timely update ensures that the client is aware of and can prepare for the additional costs associated with their case.

9.4. EFFECTIVE MANAGEMENT OF CLIENT COMPLAINTS

9.4.1. COMMUNICATING COMPLAINT PROCEDURES TO CLIENTS

When you engage a client, it's essential to provide them with clear written information about their rights and procedures for lodging complaints.

This information should include:

- **Right to Complain About Services and Charges:** Clients should be explicitly informed of their right to file complaints about the quality of your legal services or any issues related to charges.

- **Complaint Process Details:** Clearly outline the procedure for making a complaint. This includes specifying how and to whom within your firm the complaint should be directed.

- **Legal Ombudsman (LeO) Complaints:** Inform the client about their entitlement to complain to the Legal Ombudsman (LeO), including the circumstances under which they can do so. Additionally, after an internal complaint process has been completed without a satisfactory resolution, clients must be reminded again of their right to approach the LeO.

These steps are crucial in ensuring that clients are aware of their rights and the avenues available to them if they are dissatisfied with the service they receive. It demonstrates a commitment to transparency and client care, fostering trust in the solicitor-client relationship.

9.4.2. POST-COMPLAINT FOLLOW-UP

After a client's complaint has been lodged, there are specific protocols to follow if the issue remains unresolved after eight weeks:

(a) **Notifying the Client about the Legal Ombudsman (LeO):** If the client's complaint hasn't been resolved to their satisfaction within eight weeks from the time it was made, you must inform the client in writing about their right to take the complaint to the Legal Ombudsman. This communication should include the timeframe within which they can lodge a complaint with the LeO and detailed contact information for the LeO.

(b) **Exhaustion of Internal Complaints Procedure:** In cases where your internal complaints procedure has been completed and the issue remains unresolved after the eight-week period, you must clearly communicate to the client:

- That you have been unable to settle the complaint.

- The name and website of an alternative dispute resolution (ADR) approved body that is competent to handle the complaint.

- Whether you consent to engage in the dispute resolution scheme operated by that body.

9.4.3. PRINCIPLES FOR HANDLING COMPLAINTS

All complaints from clients should be addressed promptly, fairly, and without any charges to the client.

This process should be characterised by:

- **Timeliness:** Addressing the complaint as soon as possible.

- **Equity:** Ensuring a fair and unbiased review of the complaint.

- **Cost-free for the Client:** Not imposing any fees or charges on the client for handling their complaint.

9.5. GUIDELINES FOR PUBLICITY AND ADVERTISING

9.5.1. ACCURACY IN PUBLICITY

All forms of publicity related to your legal practice, including information about fees, charges, and interest on client funds, must be accurate and not misleading.

This encompasses all marketing materials, website content, brochures, and any other promotional information. The emphasis is on providing potential clients with truthful and clear information that aids their decision-making process.

9.5.2. RESTRICTIONS ON UNSOLICITED APPROACHES

- **Public Advertising:** While general advertising through public channels like billboards, radio, online platforms, or social media is permissible, there are restrictions on direct, unsolicited approaches to individuals.

- **Prohibition of Targeted Solicitation:** You are not allowed to make unsolicited, targeted approaches to members of the public to advertise legal services. This includes activities such as cold calling, direct mailings to individuals based on specific incidents, or any other forms of individual targeting.

A solicitor notices a series of articles in the local newspaper about residents experiencing issues with a new housing development project, such as construction defects or legal disputes with the developer. The solicitor then decides to send personalised letters to each homeowner in the development, offering legal services to handle their specific disputes.

This direct, unsolicited outreach to individuals based on their involvement in a publicly known issue is not allowed, as it constitutes targeted advertising to members of the public without their prior request or consent.

Exception to Unsolicited Approaches Rule:

There is an exception to the general prohibition on unsolicited approaches for advertising legal services: you are allowed to directly approach your current and former clients for the purpose of promoting your legal services. This exception is based on the existing professional relationship with these clients, which implies a level of prior consent and familiarity.

However, even in these circumstances, it's important to ensure that such communications are respectful, non-intrusive, and in line with clients' preferences and expectations. The approach should be professional and considerate of the clients' ongoing or past experiences with your services.

9.6. ADHERENCE TO SRA TRANSPARENCY RULES

The SRA Transparency Rules, introduced in December 2018, set forth specific requirements for regulated firms regarding the publication of information, especially on their websites. These rules, while separate from the Codes of Conduct, are critical regulatory mandates focusing on consumer information transparency.

Key Requirements of the Transparency Rules:

(a) **Applicable Practice Areas:** If your firm has a website and offers services in any of the following areas, you must display prices and service information:

- Residential conveyancing

- Uncontested probate

- Summary motoring offences

- Immigration (excluding asylum)

- Employment tribunals (unfair/wrongful dismissal)

- Debt recovery (up to £100,000)

- Licensing applications for business premises

(b) **Price Information:** Prices must be presented clearly and understandably. Your firm should:

- Provide the total cost, or if not possible, an average or range of costs.

- Clarify the basis of charges, including hourly rates or fixed fees.

- Indicate likely disbursements and their costs.

- State clearly whether VAT is included in the prices.

- Explain the payment structure for conditional or damages-based fees.

(c) **Service Information:** Firms must detail what is included in the quoted price. This involves:

- Specifying the services covered by the quoted price.

- Noting any services not included but which a client might reasonably expect to be part of the price.

- Providing information on key stages and typical timescales.

- Publishing details about the qualifications and experience of individuals performing the work and their supervisors.

(d) **Provision for Firms Without a Website:** For firms that do not have a website, this information should be readily available in alternative formats upon request.

(e) **Digital Badge Display:** Firms are required to display a digital badge on their website. This badge serves as an indicator of regulation by the SRA and includes a link to information about the protections this regulation offers to consumers.

#	Question	Options
1	**What must solicitors disclose when engaging in fee-sharing agreements?**	a) The agreement terms must be kept confidential b) The agreement must be documented and disclosed to the client c) Only the total amount shared must be disclosed d) Fee-sharing is prohibited e) The SRA must approve all fee-sharing agreements
2	**What is required when referring a client to a separate business?**	a) The solicitor must ensure the referral is in the client's best interest b) The client must be informed and provide consent c) The solicitor must receive a referral fee d) The client must sign a confidentiality agreement e) The solicitor must be a shareholder in the business
3	**Under what circumstances is a solicitor prohibited from making a referral payment?**	a) When the client requests the referral b) When the solicitor is acting in a criminal matter c) When the firm has an existing business relationship with the referred entity d) If the referral is for a family member e) If the client agrees to the payment

4 **What is the primary purpose of business governance in law firms?**

a) To increase profit margins

b) To ensure regulatory compliance and ethical operations

c) To promote solicitors to management positions

d) To reduce staff turnover

e) To streamline administrative work

5 **What must a solicitor do if they become aware of an impending firm closure?**

a) Notify all clients immediately

b) Ensure an orderly wind-down of operations

c) Transfer all cases to another firm without notice

d) Destroy all financial records

e) Cease operations immediately

6 **What is a Compliance Officer for Legal Practice (COLP) responsible for?**

a) Marketing strategies

b) SRA compliance within the firm

c) Overseeing client complaints

d) Financial auditing

e) Setting billing rates

7 **What is an example of an 'own interest conflict'?**

a) Representing both parties in a dispute

b) Acting for a client in a family law case

c) A solicitor having a financial stake in a business they are advising

d) Providing pro bono services

e) Representing a client in employment law

8	**When should a solicitor assess conflicts of interest?**	a) Only when the client requests it b) Only at the start of a matter c) Continuously throughout the case d) After signing the retainer
9	**When can a solicitor act for two clients with conflicting interests?**	a) If both clients provide informed consent and exceptions apply b) If they charge both clients a reduced fee c) If they work in separate departments d) If the matter involves property law only e) If the SRA grants permission
10	**How long does the duty of confidentiality last?**	a) Until the solicitor-client relationship ends b) Until the client's matter is resolved c) Indefinitely, even after the client's death d) Until the solicitor changes firms e) Until the SRA requests information

11 **What must a solicitor do before referring a client to a separate business they have ties with?**

a) Nothing, as long as the business is reputable
b) Obtain the client's informed consent
c) Provide a written disclaimer but no consent is needed
d) Only inform the SRA
e) Ensure the firm has financial interest in the business

12 **Under the SRA rules, what should solicitors do if they identify a conflict of interest?**

a) Ignore it unless a complaint is made
b) Inform all affected clients and withdraw if necessary
c) Continue representing all clients involved
d) Seek court approval to continue
e) Automatically withdraw from both clients

13 **What is the purpose of the SRA's requirement for annual return submission?**

a) To monitor solicitor fees
b) To ensure firms are complying with regulations
c) To assess law firm profitability
d) To verify client satisfaction
e) To track solicitor job changes

14 **Which of the following is a prohibited referral fee under LASPO 2012?**

a) A solicitor referring a client to a friend's business for free
b) A solicitor paying for a personal injury client referral
c) A solicitor receiving a thank-you gift from a referred client
d) A solicitor recommending another solicitor
e) A solicitor receiving referrals without any fees

15	**In what situation must client confidentiality be breached?**	a) When the solicitor believes the client is dishonest b) When disclosure is required by law c) When a colleague requests case details d) When another client inquires e) When the client requests a second opinion
16	**What should a solicitor do if a client provides unclear instructions?**	a) Proceed based on best judgment b) Seek clarification before acting c) Ignore the uncertainty and proceed d) Refuse to act on behalf of the client e) Automatically terminate representation
17	**What is the primary duty of a Compliance Officer for Legal Practice (COLP)?**	a) Managing firm finances b) Ensuring regulatory compliance within the firm c) Overseeing marketing strategies d) Handling client complaints directly e) Acting as a liaison with the judiciary

18 **How long must a solicitor maintain confidentiality of client information?**

a) Until the case is closed
b) Until the client changes solicitors
c) Indefinitely, even after the client's death
d) Only for the duration of representation
e) Until another solicitor requests the information

19 **What must solicitors do when managing client funds?**

a) Keep funds in the firm's business account
b) Maintain funds in a separate client account
c) Use client funds for office expenses if reimbursed
d) Deposit funds in a personal account temporarily
e) Transfer excess funds to the solicitor's account after a year

20 **When must a solicitor disclose their financial interest in a referred business?**

a) Only if asked by the client
b) Always, before making a referral
c) Only if profits exceed a threshold
d) If the SRA requests disclosure
e) Never, as financial interest is confidential

21	**What is an 'own interest' conflict?**	a) A conflict between two clients of a solicitor b) A conflict between a solicitor's personal interests and their duty to a client c) A conflict between two firms representing the same client d) A disagreement within a legal team e) A financial dispute between a solicitor and their employer
22	**When is it permissible to act for two clients with competing interests?**	a) Never, under any circumstances b) Only if both clients provide informed consent and safeguards exist c) If one client is more experienced d) If both clients are unaware of the conflict e) If the solicitor prefers one client over the other
23	**What is the consequence of failing to report a serious breach to the SRA?**	a) No consequence unless a complaint is filed b) Potential disciplinary action against the solicitor c) Automatic revocation of the solicitor's license d) A fine of £10,000 e) The firm being shut down immediately
24	**Which of the following is a breach of the SRA Transparency Rules?**	a) Publishing pricing details on the firm's website b) Failing to display a digital badge on the firm's website c) Offering pro bono services d) Providing a breakdown of costs to clients e) Displaying a price range for legal services

25 **What should a solicitor do if they accidentally disclose confidential client information?**

a) Inform the affected client and mitigate the damage

b) Ignore the issue unless the client notices

c) Report the incident to the police

d) Seek legal action against the recipient

e) Delete all records of the disclosure

26	**What is the primary duty of a Compliance Officer for Finance and Administration (COFA)?**	a) Managing client relations b) Ensuring compliance with SRA Accounts Rules c) Handling firm marketing strategies d) Overseeing court cases e) Providing legal training to employees
27	**What must a solicitor do before entering into a fee-sharing arrangement with a third party?**	a) Ensure it is documented in writing and disclosed to the client b) Seek court approval c) Only inform the SRA d) Charge an additional fee to the client e) Ensure it remains undisclosed to protect client interests
28	**What is the consequence of a solicitor failing to honor an undertaking?**	a) No consequence unless a complaint is made b) The solicitor may face disciplinary action c) The undertaking is automatically void d) The client must take legal action e) The solicitor can refuse to complete the promise
29	**When is a solicitor required to report an insolvency event to the SRA?**	a) Only if the firm is at risk of closing b) Whenever a solicitor or firm experiences financial insolvency c) Only if client funds are affected d) Never, as it is a private matter e) Only if requested by the court

30	**What must solicitors do regarding compliance records within their firm?**	a) Keep records demonstrating compliance with SRA regulations b) Destroy records after five years c) Store records only in digital format d) Submit all records to the SRA annually e) Only record compliance breaches
31	**When can a solicitor accept payment for referring a client to another business?**	a) Never, unless it is a regulated legal service b) Only with the client's informed consent c) Always, as long as the client benefits d) Only if the business is part of the solicitor's firm e) When the client does not ask about referral fees
32	**Which of the following is an example of a 'substantially common interest' conflict exception?**	a) Two clients investing in the same property with aligned goals b) A solicitor representing both parties in a lawsuit c) Two competitors bidding for the same contract d) A solicitor handling an inheritance dispute for siblings e) Two clients suing each other for damages

33	**What should a solicitor do if a client asks them to act dishonestly?**	a) Decline the request and consider withdrawing from representation b) Follow the client's instructions to maintain good relations c) Report the client to the police immediately d) Ignore the request and proceed as usual e) Ask another solicitor to handle the matter
34	**What is the purpose of risk management in a law firm?**	a) To proactively monitor and manage financial and regulatory risks b) To increase the firm's profit margins c) To manage staff promotions d) To ensure marketing strategies are effective e) To predict client complaints
35	**When can a solicitor disclose client information to a third party?**	a) When the third party is a law enforcement agency b) Only with client consent or when required by law c) Whenever the solicitor deems it necessary d) If another solicitor requests the information e) If the client's case has concluded

36 **Which of the following is an example of an 'own interest' conflict?**

a) A solicitor representing both parties in a divorce
b) A solicitor investing in a business they are advising
c) A solicitor representing two defendants in a criminal case
d) A solicitor handling a lawsuit against their own law firm
e) A solicitor acting for two companies merging together

37 **What action should a solicitor take if they suspect a colleague is breaching SRA rules?**

a) Report the breach to the SRA
b) Ignore it unless a client complains
c) Discuss the issue only within the firm
d) Wait until formal charges are filed
e) Keep it confidential to protect the firm

38 **What must a solicitor do before ceasing operations?**

a) Ensure an orderly wind-down that minimizes client disruption
b) Immediately terminate all contracts
c) Transfer all clients to another solicitor without notice
d) Request permission from the court
e) Ignore ongoing cases and inform the SRA later

39 **Under the SRA Transparency Rules, what information must firms publish?**	a) Pricing and service details for certain legal services b) Client testimonials c) Their internal financial reports d) The salaries of their employees e) Marketing strategies for their firm
40 **What is required for a solicitor to continue acting for two clients with conflicting interests?**	a) Informed consent from both clients and effective safeguards b) A verbal agreement with both clients c) Approval from a senior partner d) No action, as long as both clients benefit e) Permission from the SRA

ANSWERS - CHAPTERS 6-9

#	**Correct Answer**
1	b) The agreement must be documented and disclosed to the client
2	b) The client must be informed and provide consent
3	b) When the solicitor is acting in a criminal matter
4	b) To ensure regulatory compliance and ethical operations
5	b) Ensure an orderly wind-down of operations
6	b) SRA compliance within the firm
7	c) A solicitor having a financial stake in a business they are advising
8	c) Continuously throughout the case
9	a) If both clients provide informed consent and exceptions apply
10	c) Indefinitely, even after the client's death
11	b) Obtain the client's informed consent
12	b) Inform all affected clients and withdraw if necessary
13	b) To ensure firms are complying with regulations
14	b) A solicitor paying for a personal injury client referral
15	b) When disclosure is required by law
16	b) Seek clarification before acting
17	b) Ensuring regulatory compliance within the firm
18	c) Indefinitely, even after the client's death
19	b) Maintain funds in a separate client account
20	b) Always, before making a referral
21	b) A conflict between a solicitor's personal interests and their duty to a client
22	b) Only if both clients provide informed consent and safeguards exist
23	b) Potential disciplinary action against the solicitor

24 b) Failing to display a digital badge on the firm's website

25 a) Inform the affected client and mitigate the damage

26 b) Ensuring compliance with SRA Accounts Rules

27 a) Ensure it is documented in writing and disclosed to the client

28 b) The solicitor may face disciplinary action

29 b) Whenever a solicitor or firm experiences financial insolvency

30 a) Keep records demonstrating compliance with SRA regulations

31 a) Never, unless it is a regulated legal service

32 a) Two clients investing in the same property with aligned goals

33 a) Decline the request and consider withdrawing from representation

34 a) To proactively monitor and manage financial and regulatory risks

35 b) Only with client consent or when required by law

36 b) A solicitor investing in a business they are advising

37 a) Report the breach to the SRA

38 a) Ensure an orderly wind-down that minimizes client disruption

39 a) Pricing and service details for certain legal services

40 a) Informed consent from both clients and effective safeguards

#	Question	Options	
1	**What are the SRA Principles, and why are they fundamental to solicitors?**	a) They provide guidance on legal procedures only b) They outline the ethical standards solicitors must follow c) They apply only to corporate clients d) They are optional for non-practicing solicitors e) They only apply in criminal law	
2	**How does a solicitor's duty to uphold the rule of law affect their professional conduct?**	a) They must ensure laws are always enforced b) They should advise clients to challenge laws they disagree with c) They must act in a way that promotes justice and lawful conduct d) They can ignore laws that contradict their personal beliefs e) They must prioritize client wishes over legal obligations	

3	**Why is public trust and confidence crucial in the legal profession?**	a) It ensures clients never challenge legal advice b) It helps solicitors avoid liability c) It maintains the integrity of legal services and the justice system d) It allows solicitors to charge higher fees e) It only applies in regulatory cases	
4	**What does it mean for a solicitor to maintain independence, and why is it important?**	a) They should never take client instructions b) They should act without improper external influence c) They must avoid working with other legal professionals d) They must only follow the client's interests e) They are free to ignore regulatory bodies	
5	**How do honesty and integrity shape ethical decision-making in legal practice?**	a) They require solicitors to avoid misleading clients or the court b) They allow solicitors to manipulate evidence in some cases c) They permit solicitors to remain silent about client misconduct d) They only apply to written legal agreements e) They apply only when appearing in court	

6	**What are the solicitor's responsibilities in promoting equality, diversity, and inclusion?**	a) They must actively work to prevent discrimination in their practice b) They can choose not to represent certain clients c) They must only follow anti-discrimination laws if challenged d) They are only responsible for their own behavior, not their firm's e) They must provide pro bono services to all disadvantaged clients	
7	**How should a solicitor handle conflicts between SRA Principles, such as client interest vs. public interest?**	a) Always prioritize the client's interest b) Follow the principle that best serves the public interest c) Ignore the conflict and proceed as usual d) Seek client consent before applying any principles e) Follow whichever principle is easiest to justify	
8	**What constitutes unlawful discrimination in legal practice?**	a) Refusing to represent a client due to their personal background b) Setting different fees for different types of cases c) Advising a client to report discrimination d) Accepting only corporate clients e) Offering discounts to certain clients based on their background	

9	**How should solicitors accommodate disabled clients and employees to ensure fairness?**	a) By ensuring reasonable adjustments are made b) By charging additional fees for accessibility adjustments c) By offering the same services to all clients without exception d) By referring disabled clients elsewhere e) By asking clients to provide their own accessibility solutions	
10	**Why is the avoidance of abuse of position a key ethical concern for solicitors?**	a) It prevents solicitors from using their status for unfair advantage b) It ensures solicitors can charge higher fees c) It allows solicitors to advertise their personal opinions d) It ensures solicitors can refuse any client e) It ensures solicitors do not have financial conflicts of interest	
11	**How does honesty towards all parties influence client relationships and legal proceedings?**	a) It builds trust and ensures fair representation b) It allows solicitors to withhold key information from clients c) It prevents solicitors from advising on complex matters d) It means solicitors can ignore opposing parties e) It applies only in civil cases	

12	**What is an undertaking, and why is it legally binding?**	a) A non-binding statement of intent b) A promise made by a solicitor that is legally enforceable c) A casual agreement that does not require fulfillment d) A client's agreement with their solicitor e) A solicitor's personal opinion on a matter	
13	**What are some recommended practices for fulfilling legal undertakings?**	a) Always provide undertakings in writing b) Avoid making verbal undertakings c) Record all undertakings in client files d) All of the above e) None of the above	
14	**What are the common pitfalls in undertakings that solicitors should avoid?**	a) Making oral undertakings without recording them b) Providing undertakings without client approval c) Issuing vague or unclear undertakings d) All of the above e) Only a and b	
15	**How should solicitors record undertakings, and why is this necessary?**	a) In a formal log or register to ensure compliance b) Only if requested by the client c) They are not required to record undertakings d) Through verbal agreements alone e) Only for financial transactions	

16	**What are the implications of failing to honour an undertaking?**	a) It can lead to disciplinary action by the SRA b) It is legally enforceable in court c) The solicitor may face professional misconduct charges d) All of the above e) None of the above	
17	**What are the solicitor's ethical obligations regarding handling evidence and witness testimony?**	a) They must not tamper with or fabricate evidence b) They can withhold evidence if it benefits their client c) They should advise witnesses on what to say d) They can alter evidence in certain cases e) They should only provide evidence if requested	
18	**How should solicitors treat witness compensation to maintain ethical standards?**	a) They cannot compensate witnesses for giving favorable testimony b) They can pay witnesses only if they testify c) They must ensure compensation is reasonable and not outcome-based d) Both a and c e) Only a	
19	**What are a solicitor's key courtroom duties, and how should they conduct themselves efficiently?**	a) Ensure all claims are well-founded b) Avoid wasting court time c) Disclose relevant legal precedents d) All of the above e) Only a and b	

| 20 | **How do solicitors ensure adherence to court orders and disclosure requirements?** | a) By complying with all court orders in a timely manner
b) By avoiding any actions that would lead to contempt of court
c) By disclosing relevant laws and procedural issues
d) All of the above
e) None of the above | |

FINAL ANSWERS 1-20

#	Correct Answer
1	b) They outline the ethical standards solicitors must follow
2	c) They must act in a way that promotes justice and lawful conduct
3	c) It maintains the integrity of legal services and the justice system
4	b) They should act without improper external influence
5	a) They require solicitors to avoid misleading clients or the court
6	a) They must actively work to prevent discrimination in their practice
7	b) Follow the principle that best serves the public interest
8	a) Refusing to represent a client due to their personal background
9	a) By ensuring reasonable adjustments are made
10	a) It prevents solicitors from using their status for unfair advantage
11	a) It builds trust and ensures fair representation
12	b) A promise made by a solicitor that is legally enforceable
13	d) All of the above
14	d) All of the above
15	a) In a formal log or register to ensure compliance
16	d) All of the above
17	a) They must not tamper with or fabricate evidence
18	d) Both a and c
19	d) All of the above
20	d) All of the above

#	Question	Options
21	**What is the primary duty of a solicitor when handling witness testimony?**	a) To ensure all testimony supports their client's case b) To prevent the opposing party from presenting evidence c) To ensure witnesses are truthful and not influenced d) To only call witnesses who favor their client e) To avoid cross-examining their own witnesses
22	**Why is disclosure of relevant legal information to the court important?**	a) To ensure the court makes decisions based on full legal knowledge b) To give one party an advantage c) To prevent unnecessary trials d) To control the flow of evidence e) To comply with insurance requirements
23	**What should a solicitor do if a client provides unclear instructions?**	a) Proceed with their own judgment b) Seek clarification from the client c) Ignore unclear instructions and continue d) Follow the client's previous decisions e) Ask the court for guidance
24	**What is a key aspect of providing competent legal services?**	a) Ensuring services are timely and professional b) Prioritizing the firm's profitability c) Delegating work without supervision d) Limiting legal services to avoid complexity e) Only taking cases with guaranteed success

25	**What is the purpose of client confidentiality?**	a) To protect sensitive client information b) To prevent disclosure of information to regulators c) To restrict access to case files d) To ensure clients cannot be sued e) To comply with advertising regulations
26	**When can client confidentiality be overridden?**	a) If the client commits a crime or fraud b) If the solicitor disagrees with the client c) If another client requests the information d) If the case is taking too long e) If the solicitor needs the information for marketing purposes
27	**How should solicitors handle conflicts of interest?**	a) Avoid acting where conflicts exist unless exceptions apply b) Continue representing both parties if they consent c) Ignore conflicts if the client insists d) Decide conflicts based on financial gain e) Always withdraw representation in any conflict case
28	**What must solicitors do when handling client funds?**	a) Keep them separate from personal and business accounts b) Use them for firm expenses when necessary c) Transfer them to the firm's savings account d) Only document transactions over £5,000 e) Convert them into firm assets when a case is won

29	**What is the role of indemnity insurance in legal practice?**	a) To protect clients from financial loss due to solicitor errors b) To provide additional income for the firm c) To ensure all cases are profitable d) To cover personal expenses of solicitors e) To eliminate the need for client agreements
30	**What must solicitors do regarding fee transparency?**	a) Clearly communicate costs and billing structures to clients b) Increase fees when necessary without notice c) Keep fee structures confidential d) Only disclose fees if the client asks e) Offer discounts to high-profile clients only
31	**What is a solicitor's duty when supervising junior staff?**	a) Ensure they are competent and properly trained b) Allow them to make independent decisions without oversight c) Avoid interfering in their case management d) Focus on their own caseload and leave training to HR e) Only supervise if requested by the junior staff
32	**Why is risk management important in legal practice?**	a) To prevent financial instability and ethical breaches b) To maximize profits at all costs c) To ensure every case wins in court d) To avoid complaints from clients e) To satisfy marketing and advertising goals

33	**What is the purpose of the Solicitors Regulation Authority (SRA)?**	a) To regulate solicitors and enforce professional standards b) To provide funding for law firms c) To replace the role of judges d) To advocate for solicitors in court e) To create new laws and policies directly
34	**How must solicitors handle client complaints?**	a) Provide a clear and fair complaints procedure b) Ignore minor complaints c) Charge fees for handling complaints d) Only respond if legally required e) Dismiss complaints that do not affect firm revenue
35	**What is the primary purpose of the SRA Accounts Rules?**	a) To ensure proper handling of client money b) To regulate solicitor salaries c) To limit the number of legal transactions d) To simplify financial record-keeping e) To allow firms to use client money for investments
36	**When can a solicitor refuse to act for a client?**	a) If acting would breach professional obligations b) If they dislike the client personally c) If the client refuses to pay up-front d) If the case is difficult e) If the client requests urgent service

37	**What must solicitors do when engaging in referral arrangements?**	a) Disclose any financial interests to clients b) Keep referral fees confidential c) Only accept referrals from trusted firms d) Avoid documenting referrals e) Charge additional fees for referred clients
38	**What is the duty of a Compliance Officer for Legal Practice (COLP)?**	a) To ensure the firm complies with regulatory requirements b) To manage firm finances c) To oversee client cases directly d) To train new solicitors e) To issue legal rulings in client disputes
39	**How should solicitors handle professional embarrassment?**	a) Refuse to act in cases where personal values conflict b) Ignore personal feelings and continue representation c) Always disclose personal biases to clients d) Seek external approval before withdrawing from a case e) Continue acting unless a client complains
40	**What is a key responsibility of a solicitor regarding advertising?**	a) Ensure all promotional materials are accurate and not misleading b) Use any method necessary to attract clients c) Offer discounts based on client background d) Use misleading tactics to outcompete rival firms e) Avoid publicly disclosing firm services

FINAL ANSWERS 21-40

#	Correct Answer
21	c) To ensure witnesses are truthful and not influenced
22	a) To ensure the court makes decisions based on full legal knowledge
23	b) Seek clarification from the client
24	a) Ensuring services are timely and professional
25	a) To protect sensitive client information
26	a) If the client commits a crime or fraud
27	a) Avoid acting where conflicts exist unless exceptions apply
28	a) Keep them separate from personal and business accounts
29	a) To protect clients from financial loss due to solicitor errors
30	a) Clearly communicate costs and billing structures to clients
31	a) Ensure they are competent and properly trained
32	a) To prevent financial instability and ethical breaches
33	a) To regulate solicitors and enforce professional standards
34	a) Provide a clear and fair complaints procedure
35	a) To ensure proper handling of client money
36	a) If acting would breach professional obligations
37	a) Disclose any financial interests to clients
38	a) To ensure the firm complies with regulatory requirements
39	a) Refuse to act in cases where personal values conflict
40	a) Ensure all promotional materials are accurate and not misleading

#	Question	Options
41	**What is the primary duty of a solicitor when receiving client instructions?**	a) Follow them without question b) Ensure they are lawful and in the client's best interest c) Seek a second opinion before proceeding d) Always consult a barrister e) Refuse if they involve financial transactions
42	**What must a solicitor do before accepting a client's case?**	a) Ensure they have the necessary competence and resources b) Accept all cases to avoid discrimination c) Only take cases involving financial transactions d) Require advance payment before discussing the case e) Immediately refer the client to another solicitor
43	**What should a solicitor do if they identify an own-interest conflict?**	a) Continue representing the client but disclose the conflict b) Cease representation immediately c) Obtain informed consent and consider safeguards d) Refer the matter to the SRA e) Ignore the conflict and act in the client's interest
44	**Under what circumstances must a solicitor withdraw from a case?**	a) If the client refuses to pay fees b) If the solicitor lacks the required expertise c) If acting would breach their professional obligations d) If the client disagrees with legal advice e) If the case involves more than one party

45	**What is the duty of confidentiality in legal practice?**	a) It is absolute and cannot be overridden b) It does not apply to communications via email c) It requires client consent before any disclosure d) It can be overridden by law in certain circumstances e) It applies only to solicitors, not support staff
46	**When is disclosure of confidential client information permitted?**	a) If the client gives explicit consent b) If the information is widely known c) If the solicitor deems it in the public interest d) If another solicitor requests it e) If the client's spouse asks for it
47	**What is the duty of disclosure?**	a) A solicitor must disclose all client matters publicly b) A solicitor must inform clients of material facts relevant to their case c) A solicitor must report all client activities to the SRA d) A solicitor must ensure third parties are aware of case details e) A solicitor must share all evidence with opposing counsel
48	**How should a solicitor handle a complaint from a client?**	a) Address it promptly and fairly b) Ignore it unless it concerns fees c) Refer the client to another firm d) Wait for the SRA to intervene e) Charge a fee for handling complaints

49	**What must a solicitor do when a serious breach of professional standards occurs?**	a) Report it to the SRA b) Attempt to resolve it internally c) Ignore it unless the client is affected d) Inform the client only e) Seek guidance from another solicitor
50	**What is a solicitor's duty regarding misleading the court?**	a) They must always act in their client's best interests, even if misleading the court b) They must never knowingly mislead the court c) They can withhold information if it benefits their client d) They may mislead the court if the client consents e) They must consult the client before deciding
51	**What action should a solicitor take if they suspect their client is committing fraud?**	a) Continue acting unless ordered otherwise by a court b) Withdraw from representation and consider reporting it c) Ignore it to protect client confidentiality d) Notify the police immediately e) Inform the opposing party
52	**What is the purpose of risk management in a law firm?**	a) To improve efficiency in handling cases b) To identify, assess, and mitigate professional risks c) To increase firm profitability d) To manage client expectations e) To avoid regulatory oversight

53	**What is the duty of supervision in a law firm?**	a) Ensuring all legal staff act competently and ethically b) Restricting junior staff from handling complex cases c) Delegating all supervisory duties to senior partners d) Reporting all staff mistakes to the SRA e) Avoiding delegation to non-qualified staff
54	**What should a solicitor do before engaging in fee sharing with a third party?**	a) Disclose the arrangement to the client b) Obtain permission from the SRA c) Ensure it is in writing and aligns with regulations d) Only share fees with authorised professionals e) Avoid fee sharing altogether
55	**What is an undertaking in legal practice?**	a) A legally binding promise given by a solicitor b) A voluntary agreement between parties c) A solicitor's professional obligation to clients d) A discretionary commitment with no legal consequences e) A requirement for all solicitors before trial
56	**What must solicitors ensure regarding advertising their legal services?**	a) All claims must be truthful and not misleading b) Advertising must be limited to websites c) Only licensed solicitors may advertise d) Fees must always be disclosed in advertisements e) Advertising should target specific clients

57 **What is the role of a Compliance Officer for Finance and Administration (COFA)?**

a) Ensuring the firm complies with financial regulations
b) Overseeing case management for all solicitors
c) Reviewing marketing strategies
d) Handling client disputes
e) Authorising all financial transactions

58 **What should a solicitor do if a former client's confidential information becomes relevant in a current case?**

a) Seek consent from the former client before using it
b) Disclose it to the court immediately
c) Use it if it benefits the current client
d) Ignore confidentiality obligations if the case is urgent
e) Always disclose former client information to regulatory bodies

59 **What is the purpose of professional indemnity insurance for solicitors?**

a) To protect against claims of negligence
b) To fund marketing and advertising efforts
c) To provide bonuses for staff
d) To cover court costs in all cases
e) To ensure compliance with anti-money laundering laws

60 **When is a solicitor required to report another solicitor to the SRA?**

a) If there is evidence of a serious regulatory breach
b) If they suspect minor misconduct
c) Only if the client complains
d) If the solicitor is a competitor
e) Only if the solicitor refuses to correct their mistake

FINAL ANSWERS 41-60

#	Correct Answer
41	b) Ensure they are lawful and in the client's best interest
42	a) Ensure they have the necessary competence and resources
43	c) Obtain informed consent and consider safeguards
44	c) If acting would breach their professional obligations
45	d) It can be overridden by law in certain circumstances
46	a) If the client gives explicit consent
47	b) A solicitor must inform clients of material facts relevant to their case
48	a) Address it promptly and fairly
49	a) Report it to the SRA
50	b) They must never knowingly mislead the court
51	b) Withdraw from representation and consider reporting it
52	b) To identify, assess, and mitigate professional risks
53	a) Ensuring all legal staff act competently and ethically
54	c) Ensure it is in writing and aligns with regulations
55	a) A legally binding promise given by a solicitor
56	a) All claims must be truthful and not misleading
57	a) Ensuring the firm complies with financial regulations
58	a) Seek consent from the former client before using it
59	a) To protect against claims of negligence
60	a) If there is evidence of a serious regulatory breach

#	Question	Options
61	**What is the role of a Compliance Officer for Legal Practice (COLP)?**	a) Overseeing financial compliance b) Ensuring the firm complies with SRA regulations c) Managing client accounts d) Handling all litigation matters e) Setting legal fees
62	**When must a solicitor refuse to act for a client?**	a) If the client refuses to pay fees upfront b) If the solicitor lacks competence in the relevant area of law c) If the client disagrees with legal advice d) If the case involves a minor dispute e) If the client insists on going to court
63	**What must a solicitor do if they suspect a client is engaged in money laundering?**	a) Inform the police immediately b) File a suspicious activity report (SAR) with the appropriate authority c) Continue acting to gather evidence d) Withdraw from representation but remain silent e) Inform the client of their suspicions

64	**What should a solicitor do if they make a mistake that adversely affects a client?**	a) Ignore it unless the client notices b) Admit the mistake, explain its impact, and suggest remedial action c) Attempt to cover it up d) Seek advice from another solicitor before acting e) Report it to the SRA immediately
65	**What is the purpose of the Legal Ombudsman (LeO)?**	a) To regulate solicitors and barristers b) To resolve complaints about legal services c) To prosecute solicitors for misconduct d) To issue new laws regarding legal practice e) To provide free legal advice to the public
66	**What is the primary duty of a solicitor when dealing with unrepresented parties?**	a) Take advantage of their lack of legal knowledge b) Provide them with legal advice c) Ensure they are not misled or exploited d) Refer them to another solicitor e) Ignore them entirely

67	**When is it permissible for a solicitor to communicate directly with another solicitor's client?**	a) If they have the client's consent b) Only if the client approaches them first c) Never, under any circumstances d) If the solicitor refuses to communicate e) If the client is unhappy with their current solicitor
68	**What must a solicitor do when acting as an executor of a client's estate?**	a) Prioritise their own financial interests b) Follow the client's wishes and act impartially c) Charge the highest fees possible d) Seek permission from the SRA e) Act as both executor and beneficiary
69	**What is the main ethical concern when dealing with referral arrangements?**	a) Potential conflicts of interest b) The solicitor earning a lower fee c) The solicitor losing business d) The solicitor having to disclose their income e) The client choosing another solicitor
70	**When must a solicitor disclose their interest in a transaction?**	a) If there is a potential conflict of interest b) Only if the client asks c) If they are acting for both parties d) If they are financially benefiting from the transaction e) If the transaction exceeds £10,000

71	**What is the purpose of anti-money laundering regulations in legal practice?**	a) To ensure clients pay legal fees promptly b) To prevent solicitors from handling criminal funds c) To limit the number of international transactions d) To monitor all client transactions e) To prevent clients from withdrawing large sums of money
72	**When must a solicitor provide a client with a written engagement letter?**	a) Before beginning any work b) Only if the client requests it c) If the case is high value d) If the matter is particularly complex e) After the client has paid their first invoice
73	**What must a solicitor do if a client asks them to draft a will that benefits the solicitor?**	a) Proceed as usual b) Seek independent legal advice for the client c) Charge a higher fee d) Draft the will but refuse to act as executor e) Ensure the will is notarised
74	**What is a solicitor's primary duty when handling client money?**	a) Keep it in a separate client account b) Invest it for maximum return c) Use it to pay office expenses d) Transfer it to the firm's general account e) Hold it in cash

75	**What is the SRA's role in legal practice?**	a) To regulate solicitors and ensure compliance with ethical standards b) To provide legal representation for clients c) To act as a trade union for solicitors d) To set legal fees e) To handle all client complaints directly
76	**What must a solicitor do if they identify a conflict of interest?**	a) Continue acting as long as they disclose it b) Withdraw from representation unless an exception applies c) Seek a second opinion d) Allow the client to waive the conflict e) Ignore it unless the client complains
77	**What is a key duty under the SRA Code of Conduct?**	a) Acting with independence and integrity b) Maximising profit c) Following only client instructions d) Ensuring client satisfaction e) Avoiding all disputes
78	**What should a solicitor do if they receive privileged information by mistake?**	a) Read it and use it in their case b) Notify the sender and return or delete it c) Share it with their client d) Report it to the SRA e) Keep it for future reference

79	**When can a solicitor withdraw from acting for a client?**	a) Only if they have a court order b) If they have good reason and it does not harm the client's interests c) Whenever they choose d) Only if the client consents e) If the client refuses to follow advice
80	**What is the duty of a solicitor regarding the confidentiality of client information?**	a) Keep all client information confidential unless disclosure is required or permitted by law b) Share client information with other solicitors freely c) Disclose all details to the SRA d) Keep client information confidential only while representing them e) Follow client instructions about disclosure at all times

FINAL ANSWERS 61-80

#	Correct Answer
61	b) Ensuring the firm complies with SRA regulations
62	b) If the solicitor lacks competence in the relevant area of law
63	b) File a suspicious activity report (SAR) with the appropriate authority
64	b) Admit the mistake, explain its impact, and suggest remedial action
65	b) To resolve complaints about legal services
66	c) Ensure they are not misled or exploited
67	a) If they have the client's consent
68	b) Follow the client's wishes and act impartially
69	a) Potential conflicts of interest
70	d) If they are financially benefiting from the transaction
71	b) To prevent solicitors from handling criminal funds
72	a) Before beginning any work
73	b) Seek independent legal advice for the client
74	a) Keep it in a separate client account
75	a) To regulate solicitors and ensure compliance with ethical standards
76	b) Withdraw from representation unless an exception applies
77	a) Acting with independence and integrity
78	b) Notify the sender and return or delete it
79	b) If they have good reason and it does not harm the client's interests
80	a) Keep all client information confidential unless disclosure is required or permitted by law

#	Question	Options
81	**What is the fundamental principle of client confidentiality?**	a) All client information must be disclosed if requested by another solicitor b) Client information should be kept confidential unless disclosure is required or permitted by law c) Only financial details are protected under confidentiality rules d) Solicitors can discuss cases openly as long as no names are mentioned e) Confidentiality only applies while the solicitor is actively representing the client
82	**When is a solicitor permitted to breach confidentiality?**	a) If the client is involved in a minor civil case b) If there is a legal obligation, such as a court order c) If another solicitor requests the information d) If the solicitor personally believes it is in the client's best interest e) If the client has not paid their legal fees
83	**What is the purpose of legal professional privilege (LPP)?**	a) To allow solicitors to avoid answering personal questions b) To protect confidential communications between clients and their legal advisers c) To enable courts to access all client information freely d) To permit clients to discuss their cases with third parties e) To allow privileged documents to be disclosed in criminal cases

84	**What should a solicitor do if they realise they have a conflict of interest after taking on a case?**	a) Continue acting as long as the client is informed b) Withdraw from acting unless an exception applies c) Ignore the conflict if it is minor d) Inform the court immediately e) Seek advice from another solicitor before deciding
85	**What is the main purpose of the Solicitors Regulation Authority (SRA)?**	a) To regulate solicitors and ensure ethical compliance b) To offer free legal advice c) To represent solicitors in court d) To provide legal funding for clients e) To set legal precedents
86	**When can a solicitor accept a client's instructions to make a will in which the solicitor is named a beneficiary?**	a) Always, as long as the will is properly drafted b) Never, as it is always a conflict of interest c) Only if the client receives independent legal advice d) Only if the client signs a waiver e) If the solicitor does not charge for preparing the will
87	**What must a solicitor do if they receive an overpayment from a client?**	a) Transfer it to the firm's business account b) Return it to the client as soon as possible c) Keep it in the client account indefinitely d) Donate it to charity e) Use it for firm expenses

88	**What is the purpose of a client care letter?**	a) To outline the solicitor's professional background b) To confirm the terms of engagement and key information for the client c) To request payment from the client d) To provide case law references e) To ensure the client does not complain later
89	**What must a solicitor do when handling a complaint from a client?**	a) Ignore it if it lacks merit b) Respond promptly, fairly, and without charge c) Charge an administrative fee d) Wait until the complaint is escalated to the SRA e) Refer all complaints to the Legal Ombudsman
90	**What is the duty of candour for solicitors?**	a) To disclose only positive aspects of a case to the client b) To be open and honest in dealings with clients, courts, and regulators c) To withhold unfavourable information from opposing parties d) To ensure that clients never admit fault e) To share all client information with the SRA
91	**What must a solicitor do before charging a client for disbursements?**	a) Obtain the client's informed consent b) Automatically deduct the amount from the client's account c) Seek approval from the SRA d) Only charge if the total is over £500 e) Keep a percentage of the amount as a service fee

92	**What is the duty of competence for solicitors?**	a) To act in the best interests of their firm b) To provide services only in areas where they have relevant expertise c) To take on all cases regardless of experience d) To provide free services to those in need e) To follow client instructions without question
93	**When is a solicitor allowed to terminate a client relationship?**	a) If the client becomes difficult to work with b) If there is a good reason and it does not cause significant harm to the client c) Only if ordered by the court d) If they find another client who pays more e) Whenever they choose
94	**What must a solicitor do if they suspect their client is committing fraud?**	a) Withdraw from acting and file a suspicious activity report (SAR) b) Inform the client that they will report them c) Continue acting but monitor the situation d) Ignore it unless evidence is presented e) Report the client to the police immediately
95	**What is the main requirement for solicitors under the SRA Transparency Rules?**	a) To provide clear information on fees and services b) To disclose all firm expenses to clients c) To publish every case they handle d) To provide legal advice for free e) To register all client transactions with the SRA

96	**What must a solicitor do before acting for two clients in a potentially conflicting matter?**	a) Obtain informed consent from both clients b) Proceed without disclosure c) Only disclose the conflict if asked d) Prioritise the higher-paying client e) Seek a court order
97	**What does the term "fiduciary duty" mean in legal practice?**	a) A solicitor's duty to act in their client's best interests b) A requirement to always work for free c) A rule that limits the solicitor's fees d) A duty to disclose all firm activities e) A legal obligation to report colleagues' mistakes
98	**What is the role of the Compliance Officer for Finance and Administration (COFA)?**	a) Overseeing compliance with the SRA Accounts Rules b) Approving all legal cases c) Managing client litigation d) Ensuring client care letters are issued e) Setting salaries for solicitors
99	**What is the correct action if a solicitor finds out they have received confidential documents by mistake?**	a) Return or destroy the documents immediately b) Read them and decide later c) Forward them to the client d) Use them as evidence e) Keep them for reference
100	**What is the SRA's primary function?**	a) To regulate solicitors and ensure ethical compliance b) To provide free legal advice c) To manage law firm finances d) To prosecute criminal cases e) To issue court rulings

FINAL ANSWERS 81-100

#	Correct Answer
81	b) Client information should be kept confidential unless disclosure is required or permitted by law
82	b) If there is a legal obligation, such as a court order
83	b) To protect confidential communications between clients and their legal advisers
84	b) Withdraw from acting unless an exception applies
85	a) To regulate solicitors and ensure ethical compliance
86	c) Only if the client receives independent legal advice
87	b) Return it to the client as soon as possible
88	b) To confirm the terms of engagement and key information for the client
89	b) Respond promptly, fairly, and without charge
90	b) To be open and honest in dealings with clients, courts, and regulators
91	a) Obtain the client's informed consent
92	b) To provide services only in areas where they have relevant expertise
93	b) If there is a good reason and it does not cause significant harm to the client
94	a) Withdraw from acting and file a suspicious activity report (SAR)
95	a) To provide clear information on fees and services
96	a) Obtain informed consent from both clients
97	a) A solicitor's duty to act in their client's best interests
98	a) Overseeing compliance with the SRA Accounts Rules
99	a) Return or destroy the documents immediately
100	a) To regulate solicitors and ensure ethical compliance

CONCLUSION

As you conclude this comprehensive guide on Ethics and Professional Conduct, you stand on the cusp of embarking on a remarkable journey in the legal profession.

This guide has endeavoured to provide you with a profound understanding of the ethical obligations and professional standards that are integral to the role of a solicitor in England and Wales. It is designed to prepare you for the Solicitors Qualifying Examination (SQE 1) and instil in you the ethical foundation that will guide your entire legal career. Throughout these pages, you have navigated the complexities of ethical dilemmas, understood the importance of maintaining client confidentiality, learned the significance of conflict management, and grasped the nuances of professional conduct that uphold the integrity of the legal system. These lessons form the bedrock of your future practice and will serve as your compass in navigating the legal landscape with honour and professionalism.

As you move forward, remember that the legal profession is not just about knowledge and skills but also character and judgment. The ethical decisions you make, and the professional conduct you exhibit will define your career and impact the lives of those you serve. You are poised to become a custodian of justice, a role that carries great responsibility and requires an unwavering commitment to the principles you have learned.

REFERENCES

Solicitors Regulation Authority. (2019). SRA Handbook. London: Solicitors Regulation Authority.

Herring, J. (2023). Legal Ethics. Third Edition. Oxford University Press.

Kempton, J. (2021). SQE - Ethics and Professional Conduct. The University of Law.

Boon, A. (2014). The Ethics and Conduct of Lawyers in England and Wales. 3th ed. Bloomsbury Publishing.

Hammer, K. (2019) Professional Conduct Casebook: Third Edition. OUP Oxford.

Dare, T., & Wendel, B. (2010). Professional Ethics and Personal Integrity.

ABOUT AUTHORS

Anastasia & Andrew Vialichka have authored a revered collection of study guides and quizzes (metexam.co.uk), addressing the full spectrum of topics tested by the Solicitors Qualifying Examination (SQE).

Their portfolio encompasses thorough treatments of *Business Law and Practice, Dispute Resolution, Contract, Tort, Legal System of England and Wales, Constitutional and Administrative Law and EU Law, Legal Services, Property Law and Practice, Wills and the Administration of Estates, Solicitors Accounts, Land Law, Trusts, Criminal Law and Practice, Equity, etc.*

The authors' works are not only informational but also innovative, incorporating AI-based technology to enhance test preparation. This modern approach tailors learning to individual styles, aiding students to master both the theory and practice required for the SQE.

www.ingramcontent.com/pod-product-compliance
Lightning Source LLC
Chambersburg PA
CBHW061253220326
41599CB00028B/5629